Battlegroun

BATTLE OF THE AISNE 1918

Battleground series:

Battleground Europe

BATTLE OF THE AISNE 1918
The Phantom Sector

David Blanchard

Pen & Sword
MILITARY

First published in Great Britain in 2015 by
Pen & Sword Military
an imprint of
Pen & Sword Books Ltd
47 Church Street
Barnsley
South Yorkshire
S70 2AS

ISBN 978 1 78337 605 6

Printed and bound in England by
CPI Group (UK) Ltd, Croydon, CR0 4YY.

Pen & Sword Books Ltd incorporates the Imprints of Pen & Sword
Aviation, Pen & Sword Maritime, Pen & Sword Military, Wharncliffe
Local History, Pen and Sword Select, Pen and Sword Military
Classics, Leo Cooper, Remember When, Seaforth Publishing and
Frontline Publishing.

For a complete list of Pen & Sword titles please contact
PEN & SWORD BOOKS LIMITED
47 Church Street, Barnsley, South Yorkshire, S70 2AS, England
E-mail: enquiries@pen-and-sword.co.uk
Website: www.pen-and-sword.co.uk

CONTENTS

ACKNOWLEDGEMENTS

It is nearly twenty years since I started researching the Aisne battle of 1918. I was inspired to do so by the brief inscription on the front page of my great uncle's war service Bible:

> *L/Cp T Williams 9th Bn N F 9th Platoon C-Coy, 27th May 1918, 45776 Thomas Williams taken prisoner at Pontevert, released 13th November at Saaralben*

I had no idea where Pontevert, or Pontavert, was and, intrigued, found that it is near the Chemin des Dames, not far from Soissons. To cut a long story short, starting from this rudimentary piece of information, I went on to complete a research degree on the battle in 2005.

Along the way I discovered that my maternal grandfather, Private Ned Burridge, who fought with the 8/DLI, was also taken prisoner on 27 May 1918. I would like to dedicate this book to the memory of both these men who fought for the 50th Northumbrian Division until it was decimated on the morning of 27 May 1918.

I have been fortunate to have the help and support of many people through this long period of research. Charles Messenger, Steven Broomfield, John Sheen and Nigel Cave read parts – and, in Nigel's case, all – of the manuscript and I'm extremely grateful for their judicious comments, advice and support. The excellent maps in this book reflect the cartographical skills of John Plumer, Ruth Coombs and, in particular, Paul Hewson from Battlefield Design. Ian Durham, who lives in Cormicy, has been an invaluable source of local knowledge; I thank him for many conversations, which helped me open up new avenues to explore. Yves Fohlen, a battlefield guide at the Caverne du Dragon Museum and an expert on the battles of the Aisne, was also generous with his time in answering my many questions about the Chemin des Dames and Californie Plateau. I am also indebted to everyone who contributed to the Aisne / Chemin des Dames thread on the Great War Forum, which was a valuable sounding board. The wealth of photographic material in this book is testament to the kind generosity of relatives of those who took part in the battle. On a personal level, my thanks go to my partner, Michiko, and our son, Thomas, who patiently supported me in my endeavors; especially during the numerous occasions when our family holidays have been hijacked for 'urgent research'. I am also grateful of the support provided by the staff at The Liddle Collection at Leeds University, The National Archives and the CWGC for helping to further my research.

I would also like to thank the following, who helped to ensure that this publication saw the light of day: Adam Llewellyn, Alan Forster, Alan Wallace, Andrew Carrick, Andrew Gill, Andrew Rawson, Andy Jackson, Andy Pay, Angela Bird, Anne Caughey, Ann Galliard, Aris de Bruijn, Avis Holden, Bill Danby, Brian Scanlon, Christopher Noble, Chris Page, Chris White, Colin Murphy, Colin Poulter, Colin Young, Dave Taylor, David Benjamin, David Marriott, David O'Mara, David Wanstall, Denis Rigg, Elisabeth Thorn, Emma Bonney, Fae Jones, Fred Ashmore, Fred Bromilow, George De Haas, Gil Alcaix, Gill Willett, Graeme Foster, Graham Morley, Graham Stewart, Guy Smith, Helen Charlesworth, Ian Durham, Ian Wiles, James Pitt, Jane Burrell, Jean Armstrong, Jean Atkinson, Jerry Murland, Joan Paparo, John Beech, John Burrell, John Butt, John Bryant, John Massey Stewart, John Wishart, Jonathan Capewell, Keith Parsonson, Lawrence Brown, Lewis Fiddicroft, Louisa Gingell, Mr L Weaterton, Margaret Atkinson, Mark Connelly, Matthew Gilbert, Matthew Richardson, Maurice Johnson, Michelle Young, Neil Storey, Nigel Brassington, Nigel Henderson, Norman Hessler, Paul Cox, Paul Dixon, Paul Hewitt, Paul Hutchinson, Paul Kendall, Paul Seymour, Peter Hart, Peter Hastie, Peter Hurn, Pete Rhodes, Rainer Strasheim, Ralph Whitehead, Richard Flory, Richard Van Emden, Rick Vincent, Robert Brunsdon, Robert Dunlop, Robert Smith, Ron Hartley, Sebastian Laudan, Simon Barnard, Stephen Beeby, Stephen Cooper, Steve Heimerle, Stuart Wilson, Susan Tall, Terry Reeves, Terry Robson, Tim Whiteaway, William G Wood, Will Murray, Valerie Snowball.

Lance Corporal Tom Williams and brother Sam.

Private George Edward 'Ned' Burridge.

LIST OF MAPS

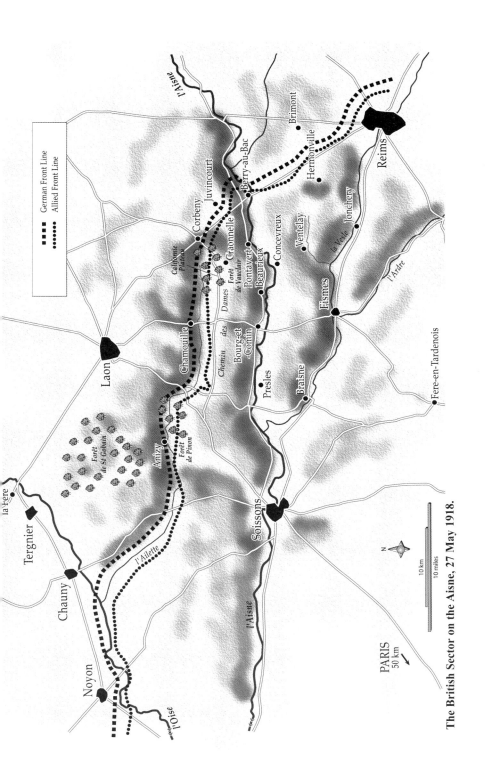

The British Sector on the Aisne, 27 May 1918.

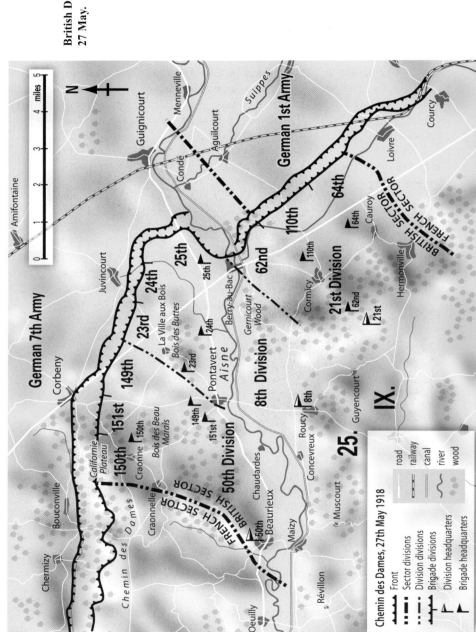

British Divisions,
27 May.

Chemin des Dames, 27th May 1918

Symbol	Description
Front	
Sector divisions	
Division divisions	
Brigade divisions	
Division headquarters	
Brigade headquarters	

road
railway
canal
river
wood

N

0 1 2 3 4 5 miles

German 7th Army

German 1st Army

Amifontaine

Guignicourt

Menneville

Suippes

Aguilcourt

Condé

Loivre

Courcy

110th

64th

64th

BRITISH SECTOR
FRENCH SECTOR

Cormicy

Cauroy

Hermonville

110th

62nd

21st

21st Division

62nd

25th

24th

23rd

25th

Juvincourt

La Ville aux Bois
Bois des Buttes

24th

Berry-au-Bac

Gernicourt
Wood

8th Division

149th

151st

Pontavert

Aisne

23rd

149th

151st

8th

Roucy

Guyencourt

Concevreux

Muscourt

IX.

25.

Corbeny

Bouconville

Chermizy

California
Plateau

Craonne

150th

Bois des Beau
Marais

Craonnelle

Chemin des Dames

150th

151st

FRENCH SECTOR
BRITISH SECTOR

50th Division

Chaudardes

Beaurieux

50th

Maizy

Révillon

Oeuilly

INTRODUCTION

The Battle of the Aisne, 1918: 'The Phantom Sector'

The 3rd Battle of the Aisne began on 27 May 1918. This German offensive, the third of 1918, was an astonishing victory – indeed, the greatest one day advance on the Western Front since the beginning of trench warfare – which also started, ironically, on the banks of the Aisne River in September 1914.

This successful operation allowed the German High Command and General Erich Ludendorff, in particular, to plan for a push on Paris,

Generalleutnant Erich Ludendorff.

some forty miles distant. The Allied armies had effectively now been split in two. The Marne was reached by 30 May, but to all intents and purpose this is where the offensive stalled.

The British IX Corps along with the French Army had stood in the way when the tremendous German barrage had ripped the front open along the heights of the Chemin des Dames plateau and across the Aisne River on the first day. This was a novel setting; one of the few times that part of a British Army was under direct control of the French. Eventually five British divisions – the 8th, 21st, 50th in the front line and the 25th and 19th in reserve – came to this haven of supposed tranquillity to rest and recuperate away from the vicissitudes of war. All these divisions had played their role in the two previous attacks on the Somme and the Lys and suffered very heavily for it. The Aisne front was a refuge. As one British soldier put it:

> *In trenches shadowed by green trees and the Bois de Beaumarais gay with flowers and singing birds, the war bore a different aspect. Here surely was the hitherto phantom sector all had one day hoped to find.*

The British divisions found resting on the Aisne in early May 1918 had

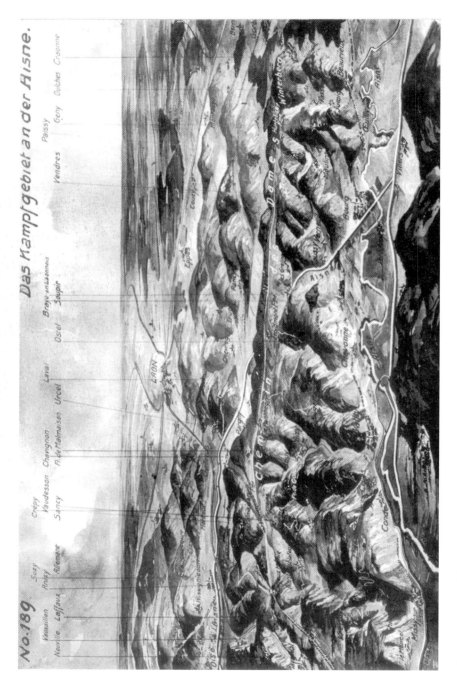

German topographical postcard of the Chemin des Dames ridges.

been part of a plan hatched by the French General Foch, which was termed "roulement". Foch hoped that relatively fresh French divisions could be transferred further north where it was felt that Ludendorff's next hammer blow would land. The British could now regroup on this rather placid sector of the Western Front. In command was the aristocratic gunner, Lieutenant General Sir Alexander Hamilton-Gordon.

At the outbreak of the war Hamilton-Gordon was major general in charge of Administration at Aldershot, a post he had been promoted to in July 1914. In May 1916, he was appointed to the command of IX Corps, succeeding Lieutenant Sir General Julian Byng. This appointment to corps commander seems to have been based solely on the patronage of the Commander-in-Chief, as he lacked the necessary experience of combat to assume such a role; and it was seen as such by contemporaries. Since February 1918 Hamilton-Gordon had been released by the General Staff to work with the French to explore the possibility of relief or intervention by British troops on the French front. In late April Hamilton-Gordon found himself charged with commanding a reconstituted IX Corps and despatched to the Chemin des Dames sector.

The 8th, 21st, 25th and 50th divisions were attached to the French *Sixth Army*, commanded by the uncompromising General Denis Duchêne. Later the 19th Division moved further south into a reserve position near Châlons-sur-Marne (renamed Châlons-en-Champagne in 1998).

Lieutenant Colonel Sir Alexander Hamilton-Gordon.

Many an infantryman who arrived on the Aisne in the warmth of an early French summer, would have concurred with Lieutenant Victor Purcell's (5th Yorkshire) thoughts:

> *For the British, who came from the bleak north, with its mud and water-logged trenches, this sector had been a haven of delight. Whereas from Ypres to St Quentin they had almost shared their parapet with the Germans, here was a No-Man's land, which gave their lungs air. In the north tons of high explosive were cast from trench to trench by mortars as easily*

Le Chemin des Dames, Decembre 1917, **F Flameng.**

> *as one would fling a stone, but here the mortars were out of range. Anywhere north of the Somme it would have been asking for trouble to have exposed a head or a hand for a moment above the parapet, but in this sector the desultory sniping from half a mile was amusement in the tranquil monotony.*

This battlefield guide and history will focus mainly on the events of the attack that fell on the British sector of the front between the 27 May–6 June 1918. The French had held this area since 1914. French monuments and cemeteries dominate the landscape. The British were also here in 1914, and they too have left reminders of their relatively brief presence. However, the actions fought here early in the war mainly occurred in the west of the sector. The battlefield of May 1918 scales the heights of Chemin des Dames Ridge, along the Californie Plateau and descends to the afforested valley of the Aisne River and canal. The retreat of the British forces during the course of the first day and in following days extends south almost to the Marne and takes in part of the Champagne region.

HISTORICAL BACKGROUND

Once a good battlefield always a good battlefield.

Rose E B Coombs

Roughly five miles to the north of the Aisne is the Chemin des Dames road. The 'Ladies' Way' was built on the order of Louis XV in 1770 to ease the carriage of his daughters, Adélide and Victoire, on their way from the Royal Palace of Compiègne to the rural residence of their former governess, the Comtesse de Narbonne Lara, in the Château de la Bove near Bouconville. The Chemin des Dames bisects an area of land referred to as *le triangle mystique*; the apex is centered on the hilltop citadel of Laon, with Soissons and Reims forming the base. Enclosed within this area, three ancient provinces of northern France meet: Picardy, Île de France, and Champagne. These three regions form a crossroads connecting Flanders – and thus much of northern Europe – with the Paris basin, and therefore most of France. Old battlefields are everywhere here. Stretching for no more than twenty-five miles east to west, the Chemin des Dames is a microcosm of this area of France that has often been referred to as the 'Cockpit of Europe'.

Julius Caesar, in his history of the war against the Gauls, mentions the capture of the fortress of Bibrax held by the Remi tribe, near present day Berry-au-Bac. Napoleon fought his last successful battle at Craonne on 7 March 1814, against a joint Prussian and Russian army under the command of Field Marshal Blücher. The Marie-Louise Monument at Le Ferme d'Hurtebise commemorates the Napoleonic legacy of 1814 and the struggle of the French *poilu* in 1914. The British Expeditionary Force fought here in September 1914 against the retreating German army. French troops, commanded by General Robert Nivelle, captured part of the Chemin des Dames Ridge from the Germans at a tremendous cost in men in 1917. In October French forces, this time under General Henri-Philippe Pétain, managed to push the Germans back even further in an audacious set piece battle at Malmaison, finally wresting the whole of the Chemin des Dames out of the enemy's hands.

By early 1918 the region had become almost a tranquil backwater. The front line still ran across the Chemin des Dames, but actual fighting was desultory; a system of 'live and let live' prevailed amongst the French and German combatants. This period of calm was shattered in May 1918, when the German Seventh Army attacked from the north.

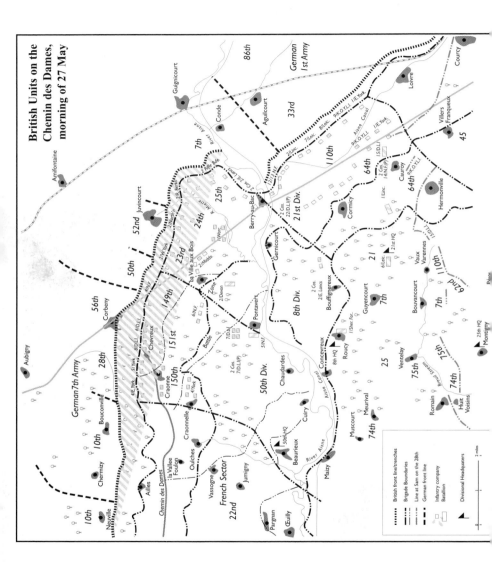

British Units on the Chemin des Dames, morning of 27 May

18

Chapter One

THE ALLIED TROOPS AND DISPOSITIONS

The sector into which the five divisions of IX Corps were posted was recognised as being one of the quietest of the whole of the Western Front, and was known to the German forces in the region as *the sanatorium of the West.* Since the French had seized the Chemin des Dames in October 1917, there had been very little activity. The French Sixth Army held a sector some fifty-five miles in length, from Noyon in the west to a point three miles north of Reims in the east. The French General Duchêne's area of responsibility had almost doubled during March and April 1918, due to the redeployment of troops to the north as a result of the German offensives.

General Denis Auguste Duchéne, GOC French Sixth Army.

The main topographic feature of the French front was the Chemin des Dames Ridge itself, which runs from the town of Compiègne in the north west to the precipitous buttress of the Californie Plateau above the village of Craonne in the east. The ridge has been compared to the chalky plateau of the Hog's Back of the North Downs near Guildford. The plateau of the

Californie Plateau and the Chemin des Dames, as seen from near Craonnelle.

3337

Chemin des Dames is a range of heights, roughly 400 feet on average, above the valley of the Aisne. The top of the plateau is gently rolling, particularly in the west between Malmaison and Braye-en-Lannois, and has a breadth of nearly three-quarters of a mile. From Californie Plateau there are commanding views to the south, where the cathedral of Reims can be observed in the distance.

The ridge appears to be a natural fortress, but in many respects this is a mere illusion. Certainly as a defensive bastion it has much to commend itself, a flat topped plateau with some severe slopes to the north and the south. Indeed, Tim Carew in his book *The Vanished Army* maintains that in September 1914 the German Army, reeling northwards after the First Battle of the Marne, came to the Aisne region and settled on the heights above the river valley and found themselves occupying a defensive position as good as any that could be found between the Urals and the Bay of Biscay. This position offered the German gunners an ideal field of fire, as well as sited battery positions and a number of old stone quarries that could be utilised as storerooms and rest areas. But the heavily wooded slopes and the river valleys of the Aisne (to the south) and the Ailette (to the north) provided cover for attackers, allowing advanced units to creep forward almost totally undetected.

The southern slopes of the Chemin des Dames, occupied by the French Army in 1918, are far from uniform. The countryside consists of gashes of limestone with sides so steep that in places the ascent is a matter of climbing on hands and knees. Although this area had been fought over for a number of months in 1917 as part of the Nivelle Offensive, deciduous woodland still covered substantial acres of the battlefield in 1918. However, the front lines running parallel with the Chemin des Dames had been badly damaged by artillery fire and the white chalk of the underlying rock strata exposed (the Germans called Californie Plateau the 'Winterberg'). The eastern sector of the French front contrasted markedly with the steep gradients of the area extending along the Chemin des Dames westwards to Soissons: east of Craonne the land drops away abruptly and for twenty miles a low flat plain extends to Reims.

The Aisne is relatively slow moving, occupying a wide fertile valley, particularly in the west near Soissons. It extends to some 180 feet in width, with many loops and meanders. Little is offered in the way of cover along the riverbank other than high grass during the early summer. Running parallel is the *Canal Lateral*, about sixty feet wide. In some places only a few feet separate the canal and river; in others the gap is up to half a mile. The river and canal are considerable obstacles to north – south movement but there are numerous bridges in the region, with fifty or more in the area from Berry-au-Bac to Soissons alone. The main bulk of the French forces were to be found sandwiched between the high ridge of the Chemin des Dames and the Aisne itself.

The staff of IX Corps reached the French front on 26 April 1918 and decamped at Fère en Tardenois, fifteen miles south east of Soissons. The first formation to arrive was the 50th Division on 27 and 28 April, and gradually over the course of the next two weeks the other divisions of the Corps arrived.

All of these divisions had played an active part in the German offensives of March and April and had suffered heavy losses as a consequence. Time was needed to refit and retrain, and the quiet sector occupied by the Sixth Army seemed to afford them this opportunity. But trained soldiers, NCOs and officers were in short supply by the early summer of 1918. The commander of the 25th Division, Major General Sir Edmund Guy Bainbridge, summed up the situation:

These reinforcements, largely composed of the nineteen-year-old class, who had been training for the last nine months in England, were most excellent material, but the absence of older men suitable for promotion to NCOs rank was, in some units, a serious disadvantage. A proportion under nineteen years of age were wisely kept back for another two or three months training. It is a thousand pities that they should have been sent from England at all. Owing to age and physique, some of these immature boys were quite incapable of carrying the weight and doing the work required of an infantry soldier in the line: their presence in the ranks rendered them a danger to their units. To use them at the time was only a waste of those who might, later on, with proper training and physical development, have become valuable reinforcements for the Army.

Unit cohesion had all but perished in IX Corps by the time these formations had reached the Chemin des Dames sector. The experience of Second Lieutenant Edwin Joicey was not untypical. In late March 1918, he was notified of his posting to France:

21

Second Lieutenant
Edwin Joicey, 15/DLI.

Arriving at Dover we saw two or three Staff Officers calling out the names of various Regiments and directing the members of each where they had to go, eventually they found several of us standing as we had not been called. One of the officers asked 'What Regiment are you?' we replied 'Northumberland Fusiliers, sir' to this the answer was 'Oh! You bloody Northumberland Fusiliers you are all alike'. We were directed to the boat and on arrival at Boulogne were taken by motor transport and confined to camp. We were there about two days before entraining to join our regiments. I, with one or two others, was instructed to report to the 15th Durham Light Infantry.

Private TH Griffiths. Originally in the West Yorks, he was transferred to the 4/Yorks, KiA aged 18, on 27 May.

By May Joicey was in command of his own platoon - he had three weeks to get to know his men before the German attack.

The Sector Held by the British

The sector that was taken over by IX Corps had been very quiet for a long time; the French and German troops stationed here had practised a live and let live system. Many of the trenches had fallen into disrepair but on paper seemed to offer many positive attributes with regard to defence.

The sector comprised three distinct positions, corresponding to the British system of a Forward Zone, Battle Zone and Rear Zone (Green Line). There were plenty of gun emplacements and many positions afforded good views over the enemy front and rear areas and the Forward Zone had a number of strongpoints all along the front, very well wired and with good deep dugouts. The Battle Zone lay a mile behind the forward positions, consisting of defended localities (often well-fortified hillocks, where battalion and brigade headquarters were stationed) and clear fields of fire for interlocking machine guns. The Rear Zone was located south of the Aisne. The defensive system was very variable here; there were plenty of trenches but no organised system of operation.

The position held by the 50th Division was 8,100 yards wide and No

Brigadier General EPA Riddell, GOC 149 Brigade.

Man's Land in this sector was considerable, up to 2,000 yards or more. The Divisional Headquarters were located in the village of Beaurieux, south of a large wood, the Beaumarais and housed in the local chateau. The area was divided into three sub-sectors, each held by a brigade plus one machine gun company. Each brigade had one battalion in the line, one in support, and one in reserve. Brigadier General Riddell of 149 Brigade provides an excellent account of the dispositions of the 50th Division, as well as the general layout of the defensive arrangements in this sector.

The sector was a most interesting one, bristling with tactical problems. In the right (149th Bde) and centre (151st Bde) sub-sectors, the ground formed a very gentle, uniform glacis slope from the Bosch lines down to the river Aisne, with seven steep sided, thickly wooded hillocks, which arose abruptly from the surrounding plain to an average height of sixty feet. A clear view of the right and centre sub-sectors could be obtained, as far as, and including, the Bosch front line and close support trenches; but the remainder of his trench system was lost to view in the woods as it disappeared behind the ridge (parallel to our front line) on which he had his front line system. From this ridge the Bosch could see every movement in our front and support lines, especially in the right sector, where movement along the trenches by day drew the fire of his snipers...The left sub-sector (held by the 150th Bde) had one outstanding feature: the famous Californie Plateau, rising abruptly to a height of 350 feet above the plain, with perhaps, half a dozen bricks to mark the site of the once beautiful village of Craonne. This extraordinary plateau stood out seared and naked, with its almost precipitous slopes disappearing as they fell to the thick woodland which carpeted the plain in every direction except south, east, and again west, where ran the Chemin des Dames.

The positions held by the 8th Division were different from those of the 50th Division in that the sector formed a right-angled salient, which projected out into the German positions. It was universally a much flatter territory, comprising an Outpost Line some 1,000 to 1,500 yards in depth as well as a Battle Zone 1,500 to 2,000 yards in depth. The front line stretched some 7,500 yards. The right flank rested on the Aisne at the village of Berry-au-Bac. This sub-sector was held by troops of 25 Brigade, with the 2/Rifle Brigade and the 2/Royal Berkshires as well as the 2/East Lancashires in the front line. The regimental history of the East Lancashires provides the following anecdote:

The line held by the battalion afforded a wide view over the back areas of the enemy's position; on one occasion a goods train was seen to draw up at a siding where large fatigue parties proceeded in broad daylight to unload it. The artillery was asked to deal with the situation, but declined to do so, pleading that they had been told not to 'disturb the peace'!

The Miette stream, roughly twenty feet wide, was located to the north and formed the boundary with 24 Brigade. This brigade occupied the central area and had troops of the 2/Northamptons and the 2/Worcester in line, with the 1/Sherwood Foresters in brigade reserve south of the Aisne. 23 Brigade was positioned on the left flank of the sector, with the 2/Middlesex and the 2/West Yorks in the front line, with the 2/Devons in reserve near the hamlet of La Ville-aux-Bois and the Bois des Buttes. 8/Machine Gun Corps had eight guns in each sub-sector and eight guns in reserve. Another notable feature of this sector was the high wooded area south of the Aisne at Gernicourt. This was a position of

Captain Sidney Rogerson, Headquarters Staff, 23rd Brigade.

some tactical strength, situated as it was on a cliff-like bastion protected by the river. A permanent garrison of 22 Durham Light Infantry (a Pioneer battalion) held the defences in Gernicourt Wood, along with troops from the 11/23rd French Territorial Battalion. Stationed in the vicinity were also French artillery and machine gun companies, all under the command of the 8th Division. Captain Sidney Rogerson, a staff officer of 23 Brigade, vividly portrays the trench system in his part of the line:

> *The ground was everywhere pitted with shell-holes, honeycombed with dug-outs and littered with tangles of barbed wire. Here were concrete 'pill-boxes' – super 'pill-boxes' – resembling square forts and all bearing the marks of artillery fire; there, in a line, the remains of seven or eight French tanks – a grim memento of the first use of these. But whereas only a year ago it had been an area of death and destruction, in May 1918 Nature had reasserted herself and hidden the grosser evidences of battle under a mantle of green. Only the actual front line trenches, dug in the chalk, seared the landscape with white scars. The woods had been blasted by the shell-fire of the previous year; but now each shattered tree stump had covered its wounds with a wealth of close foliage.*

The 21st Division held a front line position from near Berry-au-Bac running roughly south easterly for five miles and which ended near the

The Chemin des Dames and the Winterberg.

small village of Loivre, which was only three miles from Reims. The forward area of this sector was a chalk plain intersected by the Aisne-Marne canal. The front line ran east of the canal, at one point as much as 1,000 yards beyond it. This forward area lay at the foot of a densely wooded ridge, the Crête St. Auboeuf. The whole area was under view from the enemy heights, Hill 108, Mount Spin and Fort Brimont. To offset this disadvantage, camouflage netting had been set up by the French, which screened all roads and tracks for many miles. The Battle Zone lay to the west of the canal, which consisted of a chain of redoubts, which ran in front of the Laon-Reims *route national.* This area was considered to be the main line of resistance.

The trenches in this sector were very similar to those in other areas of the IX Corps front. There was too many of them. It was a complex system that resembled a rabbit warren, especially the communication trenches. The second and third lines were very badly sited and with no field of fire. These trenches were positioned on the top of ridges instead of being positioned further down the slopes (on 27 May the Germans did not bother about the ridges but went around them in every case by the valleys). The main weakness on 21st Division's front was the Forward Zone across the canal. This had been sited at the limit of the French advance in 1917. The area was very low lying, and Lieutenant Colonel Harold Franklyn (GSO I 21st Division) commented, 'I don't think 'canal' gives the right impression. Actually it was a swamp about 100 yards or more broad crossed by duck-boards tracks.'

Anglo French Co-operation

One of the most significant factors that contributed to the disaster on 27 May was the difference of opinion that existed between the British and the French as to the best defensive strategy to adopt.

The Commander-in-Chief of the French Armies, General Pétain, had laid down new principles for defensive arrangements at the end of 1917. Having observed the innovative *Stosstruppen* tactics in operation on the Chemin des Dames in July 1917; and having also taken note of German instructional pamphlets with regard to the construction of defensive positions, Pétain realised the shortcomings of the allied defence. There had to be a greater degree of flexibility; it was no longer safe to pack the Forward Zone with troops. Front line positions should be held lightly, with only enough soldiers stationed there to slow down the assaulting waves of the enemy. The main line of resistance was to be the Second Position (the British termed this the Battle Zone). This was to be the killing ground and was designed to ensure that it could not be reached by attacking troops until they had already been delayed and to be so far back as to deny them artillery support. However, support for this new 'elastic defence' was far from unanimous. General Laure, a member of the Operations Bureau of General Pétain's General Staff, pointed out what he saw as folly:

> *At the front, as in the bosom of the Government, there was stupefaction. Here was a General-in-Chief who deliberately contemplated the eventual abandonment of the famous Buttes in Champagne, conquered in 1915 at the cost of so much blood; of the advanced lines of Verdun, like Hill 304, of the heights of the Talon and the Poivre, on which were inscribed the victories of 1916; of the Chemin des Dames and the knolls of Morainvillers, the capture of which had been the only positive results of the attacks of 16th April 1917.*

Another detractor was the commander of the Sixth Army, General Denis Duchêne. He clung to the view that the defensive battle must be fought on the Forward Zone, without yielding ground. Reluctantly, Pétain gave way and approved the retention of the Chemin des Dames as a position of resistance, with the proviso, 'None of the divisions of the 6th Army placed in reserve were to be brought north of the Aisne.'

Duchêne's motives for holding on to the Chemin des Dames were purely emotional; he argued that no ground in the sector, which covered Paris, should be voluntarily given up. To do so would fly in the face of public opinion; giving up the Chemin des Dames, which had been so bitterly contested and won from the Germans the previous year, would almost have been tantamount to surrendering Fortress Verdun. A further concern may have been that the French were also reluctant to be compared to the faltering BEF (British Expeditionary Force) in the recent battles on the Somme and Lys:

> *The country would not have understood that from the experience gathered from the British front alone, a position so rich in French blood and thought to be impregnable had been given up. A certain presumption, this writer thinks, may have asserted itself in French minds: 'The English had fallen away before the enemy's great assault, but the French would stand!'*

The great weaknesses of the Chemin des Dames defence were that it lacked depth and that the Aisne, standing five miles to the rear, was a considerable obstacle. The British commander, Lieutenant General Hamilton-Gordon, and his subordinates, free from the symbolic necessity of having to hold on to the ridge, were quick to point out the shortcomings of the defensive arrangements in this area. Using the Aisne as the main line of defence, the ridge would become merely a line of outposts. In other words, this area would have been almost ideal for deploying a defence in depth.

Duchêne seems to have been loathed by most of his contemporaries although, if not admired by the troops under his command, he was respected and was given the nickname *Tigre Militare*:

> *The word was that the General was foul tempered, perpetually angry and foulmouthed for no reason. Approaching him became a form of torture for his officers, which they dared do only at the last resort. His Chief of Staff, obliged to submit to his outbreaks of anger, sulked for several days when the General went too far.*

He was not a man who would listen to advice from subordinate commanders. By contrast, Hamilton-Gordon comes across as being weak and indecisive. His dour disposition does not seem to have helped his cause, leading to him being ironically referred to as 'Sunny Jim' and 'Merry and Bright'.

The differences of opinion between the British and the French with regard to defence came to a head at a conference on 15 May at IX Corps Headquarters. All his divisional commanders, in respect of the front line dispositions of the British troops, made protests to Hamilton-Gordon. As Major General Heneker (Commander of the 8th Division) pointed out:

> This was contrary to what all the British Divisional Commanders had learnt 'up north' during the battles we had been in, viz to evacuate the forward zone out of trench mortar range.

These protests were relayed to the French Commander, who replied, 'You English have learnt up north how to retreat, I will teach you to stand.'

This sorry situation placed Hamilton-Gordon in an awkward position. In charge of a relatively small force under a French commander of higher rank on French soil, he could do little but register his protests to GHQ. It was too little and, in the event, too late for those troops enjoying much needed respite from action until the last week in May in what was a tranquil and placid sector.

Major General Sir WG Henneker, GOC 8th Division.

Royal Engineers from the 50th Division newly arrived on the Aisne, May 1918 (Helen Charlesworth).

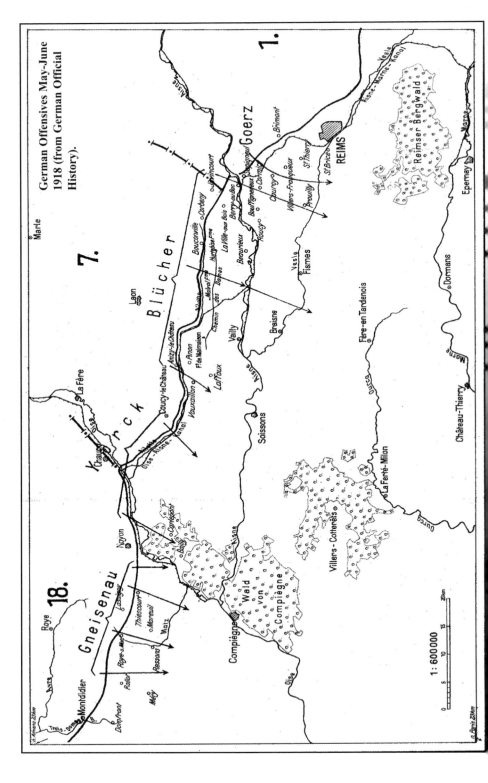

German Offensives May–June 1918 (from German Official History).

The German Plan and Preparations

For more than a month Ludendorff had been planning an attack across the Chemin des Dames. Operation Blücher, named after the famous Prussian Marshal from the Napoleonic era, was only to be a diversionary attack. After the German army had surmounted the steep ridge above the Aisne, they would press on to the Marne. Ludendorff anticipated that the French would panic and transfer all reserve forces from the Flanders region to cover what they believed would be a direct assault against the French capital. Having in effect divided the Allied armies, the main blow of the attack would be launched against Haig's forces in the north. Preparations would demand almost total secrecy to achieve the operational surprise that was required for success. The attack was to take place on 27 May 1918.

Gebhard Leberecht von Blücher in Laon, 1815.

A thirty-five mile front between Soissons and just to the north of Reims was selected as the prime focus of the offensive. Two Armies were to be responsible for delivering this attack. The German Seventh Army, under the command of Generaloberst Max von Boehn, was tasked with the main assault, with subsidiary support on the easterly flank from the First Army under General der Infanterie Fritz von Below. The Seventh Army consisted of six corps, two of these, under the command of General Richard von Conta (IV Reserve Corps), and

31

General Graf von Schmettow (LXV Corps), faced the British contingent. Some forty-one German infantry divisions were massed along the front. The Allies in comparison had nine weak divisions from the French Sixth Army as well as three from the depleted British IX Corps.

Preparation for the offensive was meticulous. All movement was confined to the dark of night. Nature helped to contribute to the concealment. The area between Laon and the front line was in places heavily forested, it was spring and the trees were in full leaf. This region proved ideal in providing storage depots for the vast amounts of ammunition and other supplies that were required for the operation.

General Max von Boehn, commanding the German Seventh Army.

The mating sounds of thousands of frogs in the Ailette valley also helped to mask the sounds of troops, supplies and ammunition being ushered forward. The wheels of all vehicles on the move were well-greased and even fitted with leather coverings, iron-rimmed wheels were padded with tyres of wool-wood or rags, and every artillery piece with loose metal was wrapped in straw. Even horses' hooves were padded with cloth. Additionally, no vehicle on road or rail displayed a label or any other distinguishing feature.

Artillery was to play the decisive role. Much depended on the fire plan of Oberst Georg Bruchmüller, the master gunner technician of the earlier German offensives of March and April. Some 5,263 guns were to be used against the Allies' 1,422 – the greatest superiority ratio achieved by the Germans in any of their battles during the course of the Great War. Ludendorff had total faith in his artillery commander and as a mark of respect he made Bruchmüller artillery chief of Crown Prince Wilhelm's Army Group shortly before the battle commenced. One of the innovations for this battle was that guns and trench mortars were to use only gas shells for the first ten minutes. This was designed to create panic and to demoralise right from the start. The next phase of the barrage consisted of a bombardment of mixed gas and high

Oberst Georg Bruchmüller, commanding German Seventh Army Artillery.

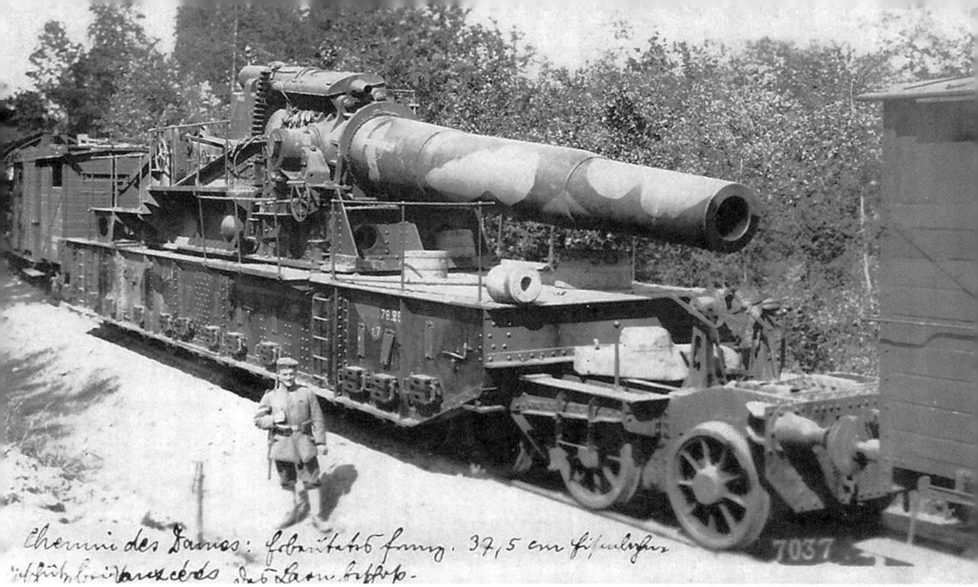

German railway gun used in the attack on 27 May.

explosive targeted at French and British artillery positions, as well as mortar shelling of front line defences. In total the artillery preparation lasted two hours and forty-five minutes, the shortest but the most concentrated of any of the German attacks of 1918.

In the days running up to the battle confidence on the German side remained high. Major General AD von Unruh, Chief of Staff of von Conta's IV Reserve Corps, had carried out a detailed reconnaissance of the sector occupied by British troops and helped plan the German assault on Californie Plateau. He was summoned before Ludendorff and asked what he expected would be the extent of the German advance on the first day. He had no doubts. He predicted that German troops would reach the Vesle River, some twelve miles to the south. This would mean that the Chemin des Dames and the Aisne would be in German hands by the afternoon of 27 May: 'Our preparations were so thorough that, if the information of their weakness in numbers was correct, we should overrun the English.'

Corporal Adolf Hitler, of the 16th Bavarian Reserve Infantry List Regiment, later recalled his experiences on the eve of the battle:

We set off for the second offensive in 1918 on the night of the 25th. On the 26th we spent the night in a forest, and on the morning of the 27th we prepared for duty. At 5 o'clock in the morning we departed. The day before, during the afternoon, we received reinforcements for the big offensive at the Chemin des Dames.

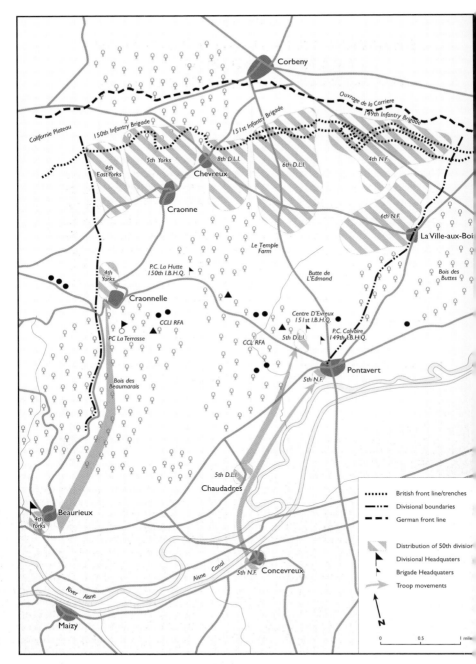

The 50 Division on the eve of battle.

Chapter Two

THE DEFENCE OF THE CHEMIN DES DAMES AND CALIFORNIE PLATEAU: THE 50TH (NORTHUMBRIAN) DIVISION

150 Brigade

The extreme left of the British line on the morning of the attack was held by 150 Brigade of the 50th Division. The battalions of the brigade had suffered severely in both the March retreat on the Somme and the Lys battle, and by May there had been a very considerable change in personnel. One officer reported that by the end of the Aisne fighting he was the only officer remaining from the battalion serving with it before March. Brigadier General HC Rees, the GOC, was equally concerned about the lack of experience of the officers in the brigade, as well as the disposition of the troops even before the Aisne fighting began.

The company officers were completely untrained, almost without exception. The simplest orders were misunderstood, whilst the

Brigadier General Hubert C Rees (left), commanding 150 Brigade, standing next to Major General G Carter-Campbell.

frontage allotted to the division, some 11,000 yards, reduced the force to a minimum.

The French 22nd Division held the remainder of the Chemin des Dames as it stretched away to the west. The 4th East Yorkshire Regiment (4/East Yorks), along with the 5th Yorkshire Regiment (5/Yorks), occupied the flat-topped, but steep sided, Californie Plateau and the front line village of Craonne (a distance of 2,600 yards), with the 4th Yorkshire (4/Yorks) in brigade reserve between the villages of Craonnelle and Beaurieux, the latter housing divisional HQ.

The 4th East Yorkshire Regiment: 'The Hull Rifles'

When the attack began at 1 am, the East Yorkshire were the left hand battalion of the brigade, and had A Company in the front line, B Company in immediate support in Trench Falaise, C Company in Craonne and D in support in P C Marais. The front line was dangerously thinly held, whilst many of the senior NCOs were away on divisional instruction courses or on leave. This added to the tragedy of the first day; it was in these circumstances that experience was desperately needed to help stiffen resolve and provide the necessary organisation for those troops who were in action for the first time. There were also problems with the supply of ammunition; no British grenades (often called bombs at the time) were available, only those grenades left behind by the French, which proved extremely difficult to detonate.

Major Horace Haslett, 1/4 East Yorks, attached from Royal Irish Rifles. Taken prisoner on the morning of the attack.

In fact there was very little chance for the men of this battalion to retaliate. Throughout the initial phase of the bombardment a high percentage of the men were killed or badly wounded. Major HR Haslett of 4/East Yorks (attached from the 9th Royal Irish Rifles) records:

> *During the bombardment, I managed to get to and from the Headquarters of the front line, and support Companies, but found*

that, with the exception of the few men in the Company dugouts, the remainder had been entirely wiped out, the suddenness and weight of the bombardment having evidently killed any men on duty in the actual trenches.

The bombardment was certainly considered the heaviest ever experienced by men who had been through previous shows. Inside ten minutes of the commencement, communication was completely cut between Battalion H.Q. and Brigade and between Battalion H.Q. and the companies in front.

German troops cross the Ailette stream in the early hours of 27 May.

Haslett and a wounded sergeant major were captured with their empty pistols in their hands.

This cataclysm was a fate that few British battalions escaped during the first few hours of the attack. Private Tom Eastham, from Preston, writing to a comrade's parents some time afterwards, testifies to the severity of the German attack on the plateau:

At 12.30 their guns started to bombard our trenches and I went out on sentry, and Robinson went on guard over the Lewis gun. He kept up a heavy fire at the advancing

Private Robinson Batey, 1/4 East Yorks, wounded and taken prisoner.

37

Germans, and had terrible revenge on them, as they were coming in thousands. About 2.30 a large shell exploded just in front of the Lewis gun and Robinson got hit with a piece. I thought he was badly hurt, but two of the lads took him down in a deep dug out and I stayed with the gun until it was put out of action. I then went to see if Robinson was alright, and was surprised to see him walking about, and he said he was a lot better. At about 4.30 the Germans made a big effort, and started driving us out of the trenches. Then Germans came into the dug-out for shelter as their own guns were still battering our trenches, and we had a tussel (sic). One of our men killed them with a bomb.

German soldiers of the 109 IR on Californie Plateau with prisoners from 150 Brigade.

I said 'It's no use stopping here, let's get out of it.' There were eleven of our lads wounded and I was the only one not wounded. They advised me to try and get away as we would soon be surrounded, so I came out and made a dash for it, and heaven knows how I got away. I was wounded in the leg and gassed and taken into hospital.

Lieutenant J F Stevenson, Royal Irish Rifles, attached 1/4 East Yorks. Captured 27 May.

CQMS William J Jackson, 4/Yorks.

The East Yorkshires (the few still remaining at their posts) were aware that at 3.40 am the German infantry attack would begin, but they did not expect an assault on both flanks. Craonne and Californie Plateau were enveloped by German troops (at approximately 6.30 am) advancing on the right flank of the divisional front and through the French division on the left. The enemy had effectively got behind the battalion and observation, which was difficult with the continued shelling, worsened when the battalion's ammunition dump on the rear slope of the plateau was set alight.

According to the unit's War Diary, the battalion was completely disorganised. A few isolated rearguard actions were fought before the majority of its men were overwhelmed and taken prisoner. Some few individuals managed to cross the Aisne in the late morning and join up with CQMS William Jackson, of the 4/Yorks, and the transport details in an attempt to defend the bridges at Maizy. However, the enemy proved too strong and much equipment, stores, vehicles and even the battalion records were abandoned in the hasty retreat. The bleak situation was recorded in the last entry in the Battalion War Diary for the period 28/31 May (the days were run into each other):

> *Ceased to act as a battalion, but remnants of brigade details acted as a composite battalion under the command of Lieut.-Colonel N W Stead. Total strength representing this battalion, four officers and 105 other ranks.*

Lieutenant Colonel Stead was the only commanding officer of the brigade left on active duty after the first day; the others were killed or taken prisoner. Everard Wyrall concludes this section in his history of the East Yorkshire Regiment by stating that both the 1st and the 4th Battalions had been practically wiped out. Twenty officers of the 4th alone were taken prisoner, whilst there is no record of how many other ranks ended up in German hands.

Lieutenant N W Stead 4/Yorks, April 1915. Later Lieutenant Colonel N W Stead, CO, 1/4 East Yorks, May 1918.

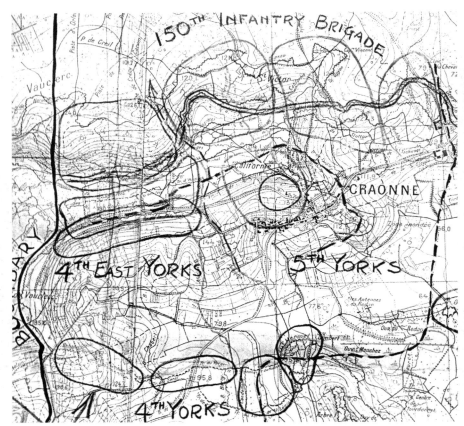

150 Brigade sector.

The 5th Yorkshire Regiment (The Green Howards)

The 5th Yorkshire Regiment (5/Yorks) was positioned to the right of the 4/East Yorks, with three companies occupying the front line (A, B, C Companies) and one in reserve (D Company). Its headquarters were located in Craonne, along with the CO, Lieutenant Colonel J A R Thomson. He was a man, according to Sir Arthur Conan Doyle, writing in his *History of the Great War*, 'worth half a battalion in his own person upon the day of battle'. As information filtered through to units in the front line that a German attack was expected in the early hours of 27 May, a reserve company of 4/East Yorks was placed at the disposal of Thomson.

The opening German bombardment, which began precisely at 1 am, on Californie Plateau and around Craonne obliterated the front line trenches and the dugouts of the battalion in an equally destructive

40

Private George Boshier, 1/4 East Yorkshire, KiA 27 May (bottom right).

fashion as those of 4/East Yorks – perhaps even more so. Communications with neighbouring units were lost, although a buried cable remained intact, allowing some contact with Brigade Headquarters to be maintained for a period of time. Attacked from both flanks by German infantry units at 4.30 am, an attempt was made to drive the enemy from the plateau by the reserve, D Company and the company of East Yorks that had recently been assigned to the battalion.

German troops from III battalion 109 IR on Californie Plateau, morning 27 May.

The ascent up to the line from the dugouts for these reserve companies was very steep and the counterattack attack failed with heavy casualties. At the same time Brigadier General Rees ordered a company of 4/Yorks, commanded by Captain A L Goring, under his direct control at Brigade HQ at La Hutte, to attack in flank the enemy who

Lieutenant Colonel JAR Thomson, commanding 5/ Yorks, KiA 27 May.

Corporal Thomas EM Lyon 5/Yorks, PoW 27 May. After the war he became billiards champion of Yorkshire.

were advancing against 5/Yorks through Craonne. This attack, which might have extricated 5/Yorks, was swept away by the tremendous barrage of shell fire falling around Brigade HQ.

Lieutenant Colonel Thomson was killed in this action; in his last message to Rees, at about 5.45 am, he said that his headquarters company was fighting around his command post and that they appeared to be surrounded:

'I'll say goodbye, General. I'm afraid I shall not see you again.' I said, 'Try to escape, the British army cannot afford to lose you.' I subsequently heard that after fighting to the last he ran for it and was killed… He was one of the finest characters I've met.

After these counter-attacks failed, Rees ordered the remnants of 5/Yorks to try to break through to the rear, but very few men managed to do this successfully. The details in the War Diary for 27 May are very scant, *'Enemy attacked at 4.30 am. Barrage commenced at 1 am.'* Then follows a list of missing officers by name, in all twenty-five. Nine other ranks are reported as killed with another 638 missing. Less than a hundred men from the battalion reported for action. As things became clearer, the battalion suffered eighty-eight men killed on 27 May, the remaining missing casualties, wounded and unwounded, being taken prisoner. Casualties were so heavy that the battalion was not reformed for the rest of the war.

The 4th Yorkshire Regiment (The Green Howards)

The story of 4/Yorks in March and April 1918 is broadly similar to that of her two sister battalions in 150 Brigade. Severely depleted in men by the end of April, the battalion received drafts of twenty-three officers and 802 other ranks as replacements in early May. Lieutenant Colonel Ralph Dawson Kent commanded the battalion. Kent was a controversial man; he had been responsible for ordering a premature attack by his company (A) of 7/Yorks at Fricourt on 1 July 1916. This was strictly against orders, as the battalion's role had been to hold the line. His company had attacked with 140 men; 108 became casualities due to Kent's tragic mistake. Despite this action, Kent, wounded on the Somme, worked his way back to France via the Training Reserve and was promoted to major. According to the battalion War Diary, of the 4/Yorks, entry for the 14 April 1918: 'Major R E D Kemp (sic) reported for duty and assumed command of the Battalion.'

In some ways it was a strange appointment, but the rate of attrition for senior officers, particularly in the 50th Division during the German offensives of the spring of 1918, goes some way to explain this anomaly. The 5/Yorks had lost both the CO and Adjutant on the 22 March. Other experienced officers had been killed or seriously wounded in April.

The battalion was in reserve near the 50th Division Headquarters at Beaurieux when orders came through during the early evening of 26 May that an attack was to take place the next morning. However, it appears that there was no immediate sense of urgency when the companies of the battalion were ordered to fall in within the hour:

> *In a short time the narrow street of Beaurieux was full of men and horses competing for possession. Companies fell in platoon by platoon whilst sergeants called out names. The men were not in a hurry and scouted the idea of anything happening in that quiet front… Concerning the attack there was general incredulity. When the battalion had stood to all night in an open trench and zero hour had been as still as the dead, they would march back to billets exhausted. A company bomber expressed the common feeling, "They're takin'oos oot to see t'stars," he said.*

Two companies under the command of Kent moved into trenches just north of Craonnelle, to the British Battle Zone at Mount Hermel. The Battle Zone consisted of strongpoints and defended redoubts, situated about a mile behind the front, which was generally of less depth, relying on the enfilade fire from machine guns. The strongpoints were often small knolls, like Mount Hermel, found on spurs of land projecting at right-angles from the ridge of the Chemin des Dames. The remaining two companies were commanded by Major L Newcombe. One moved into Brigade reserve at La Hutte, whilst the other moved north and was positioned between 5/Yorks on the right and linked up with another company of 4/Yorks on the left, in the British Battle Zone. By 11 pm all the companies were in position. The adjutant of the battalion, Lieutenant (Acting Captain) Victor Purcell, in his autobiographical novel, *The Further Side of No–Man's Land*, provides a vivid insight into the preparations made by his unit on the eve of the attack:

> *The number of rounds of ammunition served out to each man was increased from 120 to 170, and a carrying party laboured under the load of boxes of SAA, which they dumped at the store at the junction of two communication trenches leading to the front line; Mills bombs, ready detonated, were in bags and boxes along the fire-step, at hand when they should be required. Connection was established with the Windleshires [5/Yorks] in front, the French on the left, and the battalion far away over the plain to the right [8/Durhams]. The second in command, with an orderly, went to visit the three companies in direct support. The routine progressed steadily.*

Despite the appearance of smooth working, the trenches in the Battle Zone were inadequate:

> *The reserve line was only occupied on such occasions such as the present, and its dug-outs were few and not in good repair. The attempt on the part of ten signallers and as many men to occupy a dark cavern five feet by seven brought forth muffled oaths from the sepulchral depths, as if the dead of some ancient catacombs had suddenly come to life and complained of overcrowding. It was with the utmost difficulty that the parties crammed into the various holes that could be found. As for the regimental sergeant major, a man skilled in these matters, he viewed the two layers of sandbags covering his retreat and was dubious. "Wouldn't stop a pip-squeak," he said.*

Victor Purcell described the German bombardment in the sector occupied by 4/Yorks. Although not subject to as intense a barrage as along the front line, the battalion and brigade headquarters in this reserve position had also been carefully targeted by the enemy.

The parapet was knocked in all along the trench and the fumes of phosphorus rose from the charred earth. At one place, where the trench was blocked, carrying parties and stretcher bearers had to go above ground and were exposed to their thighs in the long grass. The roof of a dugout near headquarters, occupied by signallers and runners, received a direct hit from a 9-inch [shell] and had subsided, imprisoning those within. A corporal and three men worked away with spades at the entrance like men possessed and, regardless of the shells bursting near them, of singing nose-caps and jagged pieces of shell case ripping the sides of the sandbags, they dug until they could lever the fallen girders and get at the men.

Lieutenant (Acting Captain) Thomas Wiggins, 4/Yorks, KiA 27 May.

One of the immediate effects of the shelling was that the telephone wires were cut and, although linesmen were sent out to restore communication, Lieutenant Colonel Kent at Mount Hermel had to depend on runners. By 4.30 am large numbers of German troops were spotted on the move from the north west and pouring over the hillside from the Plateau de Casement, which was held by the French 22nd Division.

Brigadier General Rees decided that the three companies of the rest of the battalion – apart from one company that had been dispatched to help 5/Yorks, clinging on to Californie Plateau – stationed north of Craonnelle should stay in position. Rees's assistant staff captain, Thomas Wiggins, relayed the information to Kent, and thus from 6 am 4/Yorks were effectively holding the front line. Wiggins turned to go back to brigade but never reached it. He had just set off down the trench when machine gun fire from an aircraft struck him in the back and he fell on his face, dead.

Shortly after this, about 6.15 am a group of men were seen running and stumbling, moving in open ground away from Craonne. This was the remnant of C Company falling back. German machine gunners began to target the remaining companies of 4/Yorks at Mount Hermel from the direction of the village. On the other flank German troops were observed moving closer from the direction of the sector formerly held by the French 22nd Division. It was not long before a bombing contest ensued on this flank, with men of the Yorkshires raking down earth from both sides of the trench in an effort to shore up a communication trench and block the penetration of the enemy bombers. An eyewitness to this action, Private George Wiles, adds the following:

We had no sooner reached the trenches than the Germans started bombarding us with high explosives and gas shells. We had our gas masks on for over six hours and we were not in a very fit state when at last we were able to take them off. As soon as dawn came the Germans started to advance and came over in thousands. The bombardment grew terrible and our men were being killed and wounded on all sides.

Our Colonel Mr Flint [sic – Kent] ordered us to hold on at all costs, and at last the enemy started to bomb us and I was blown over the parapet and wounded in both heels. Mr Webb (our acting adjutant) was seriously wounded by a rifle bullet and told us to retire. As we were preparing to leave the trench, one of the enemy fired his rifle at me point blank and the bullet went through my left ear. I fired at him and saw him fall and then I went after the others down the communication trench with the enemy coming on pretty fast behind. As we were going down this trench a bullet caught me in the back and I was told by the colonel to go to the dressing station. A chum and I set off together and managed to

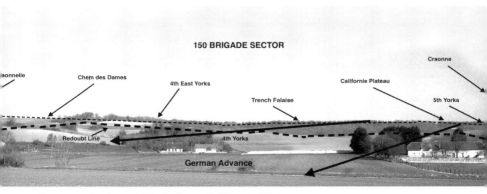

German attack on 4/Yorks from Californie Plateau.

get through the barrage. When we reached the dressing station we found it empty and had to scramble on to another one.

Wiles was taken prisoner later that day near Fismes.

Major Newcombe, arriving from Brigade Headquarters at 6.40 am, witnessed the by now desperate nature of 4/Yorks' defence of the Battle Zone:

On my return journey to Battalion H.Q. I noticed that the enemy's barrage had lessened very considerably and that I was several times fired on by machine guns and rifles at quite close range. This fire was coming from both flanks. On reaching Battalion H.Q. I found a party of the enemy in the neighbourhood of the H.Q. about 20 strong – officers, cooks, signallers, scouts, and runners and batmen – were turned out. We retired under close fire about 200 yards down a communication trench. Enemy bombing parties were held up here for some fifteen minutes, then we had to retire to Craonnelle as we were attacked also from both flanks.

A few more stragglers were collected by Newcombe en route to Craonnelle:

Found them at the bottom of the trench looking blank, with their backs to the parapet and their bayonets stuck in the duck-boards. Not every man was a fighting unit on that 27th of May. Amongst the reinforcements were men and boys straight from England, with next to no training and no conception of war. Here they were

The ruins of Craonne village and the slope leading up to the Chemin des Dames, March 1916.

French Sector

4th East Yorks

La Terrasse

Chemin des Dames

German Advance

Craonnelle

4th Yorks

German attack towards Craonnelle.

enduring their first shock of action. Many had risen to the occasion, others who were stupefied, would later on, if they were spared, show that they too could be soldiers.

Two Lewis guns were placed in the rubble of houses on the outskirts of the village. Captain Purcell was in the thick of the action:

One Lewis gun fired over a pile of bricks on the left, and a corporal took the other through the ruins and fired from a window-gap in the front. The riflemen kept up a steady fire from both sides of the building. No bullet was without a mark. There seemed to be shoals of grey coated infantry and machine gunners, getting what cover they could in the unevenness of the ground.

This was indeed a motley crew, none more so in appearance than Lieutenant Colonel Kent:

The Colonel, usually the most regimental in his costume, now for some inexplicable reason had taken off his shrapnel helmet and tied a gay bandanna handkerchief round his head. Perhaps he sought comfort in this extremity. Now he looked more like a Mexican chief than a battalion commander.

Newcombe takes up the story:

We held on here for about a quarter of an hour, by which time the enemy in front had advanced to within 200 yards of our position. We were also being fired on from both flanks and cavalry was coming up the road from Craonne. A field gun firing at point-blank range also opened fire. Only five got out of Craonnelle, the remainder being killed or captured.

Corporal Alfred C Anderson, 4/Yorks. His company was overrun by the German advance and he and a small group were taken prisoner from a shell hole behind enemy lines at 5 am. Imprisoned in Quedlinburg Camp.

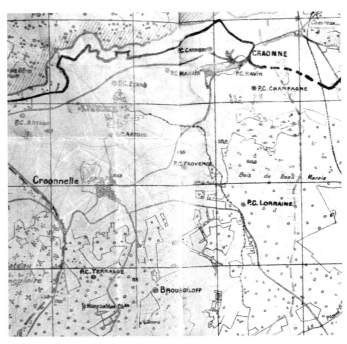

French Map showing PC Terrasse (south of Craonnelle) where Brigadier General H C Rees was making for on the morning of the attack.

It is not certain if Kent was also killed at Craonnelle, or was mortally wounded whilst attempting to fall back to a defensive position to the south at La Terrasse. Newcombe's account is not clear: '*The CO had been mortally wounded, one man hit in the leg, and the rest of us, having no rifle ammunition and only a few rounds of revolver ammunition, were captured.*'

German Artillery descending the Californie Plateau Notice British PoWs from 150 Brigade

The Kaiser and Brigadier H C Rees, Chemin des Dames, 28 May.

At about the same time Rees had left his Brigade Headquarters at La Hutte and was moving towards 4/Yorks at Mount Hermel to get a closer view of the battle. However, he and an orderly were still some five hundred yards from Mount Hermel when they observed that the Yorkshires were being overwhelmed by German forces. Rees determined to make his way to PC Terrasse, to rendezvous with Brigade Headquarters, who had been directed earlier by him to move to this reserve position. However, the German advance had moved on apace and PC Terrasse was virtually surrounded. Rees managed to extricate himself from this position, but was captured a couple of hours later whilst trying to cross the Aisne. Early the next morning, 28 May, Rees was driven by car back to the Chemin des Dames Ridge. There he was granted an audience with His Imperial Majesty the Kaiser, who had come to witness the success of his offensive at close hand.

Brothers William W and Herbert Constantine (second row, second right and front row right) at pre war training camp of 4/ Yorks. Herbert was killed on the morning of 27 May (Simon Barnard).

150 Brigade, except for the rear details, who had been left out of the trenches, had effectively ceased to exist. Brigade Headquarters was not reformed until a couple of days later, on 31 May, at Vert la Gravelle, some thirty miles to the south of the Aisne. Nearly sixty officers from 150 Brigade alone were led off into captivity.

151 Brigade

The effect of the German bombardment on 151 Brigade was catastrophic. The British positions occupying the lower ground to the east of Californie Plateau were overrun by the German attack divisions early in the morning of 27 May, allowing the main thrust of the German infantry to penetrate the Chemin des Dames. The enemy artillery targeted all of the key communication centres in 151 Brigade's sector and, within an hour, the most vital links of this network had been broken. Brigade Headquarters at Centre d'Evreux lost communication

German infantry pour over the Chemin des Dames on the first day of the offensive.

with Divisional Headquarters within the first fifteen minutes of the commencement of the bombardment – this was never restored. Battalions within the brigade were equally affected, especially the two units in the front line, 8/DLI and 6/DLI. These battalions lost direct telephonic communication with the brigade shortly after 2 am.

8 Durham Light Infantry

8/Durhams held the left-hand position of the brigade sector. 8/DLI had spent many industrious days prior to the attack strengthening their part of the sector. Trenches were improved, those open to view were protected by camouflage netting, while others were deepened and cleared of undergrowth. As the maps of the trenches were found to be inaccurate, these, after careful reconnaissance, were corrected. Saps in the front line were extended into No Man's Land along the Craonne-Corbeny road.

Two important small hills, Chevreux and Lamoureux, offered views over the German positions in Corbeny. Lamoureux hill, in particular, was a good tactical position, offering a field of fire to the right across the plains as well as to its immediate front. A series of small redoubts were strengthened in the Battle Zone occupying the northern edge of the Bois de Beaumarais. This was a large wood that extended throughout 151's sector almost from the Aisne to the Forward Zone.

At 1 am, as predicted, the German bombardment began. Captain Ernest Veitch, at that time attached to 149 Brigade HQ and the future historian of 8/DLI, observed:

> *Gas shells fell over the whole area, but were concentrated on the Battalion and Brigade Headquarters. Within fifteen minutes all communication by telephone with Brigade Headquarters failed and by 2 am also failed forward of Battalion Headquarters to the companies. Only two of all runners who endeavoured to reach the Brigade from either of the 6th and 8th Battalions, a distance of about 800 yards, succeeded and those bearing a message timed 3.30 am only arrived there at about 7 am.*

Despite the assiduous preparations made by the infantry companies to improve trench fortifications in this sector, by 3.30 am the opening salvos of the German barrage had levelled the front line trenches held by D Company, under the command of Captain J Hutchinson. Only the most forward posts remained. The casualties in these trenches were appallingly heavy. B Company, on Lamoureux Hill, suffered the same fate. The battalion's history notes that not a single officer or man escaped from either of these forward companies. Captain Robert Wharrier called his remaining officers together and they decided to fight to the last. However, the Germans, following up quickly on the

Front line positions held by B and D Coy 8/DLI, with support from C Coy 7/DLI, morning 27 May.

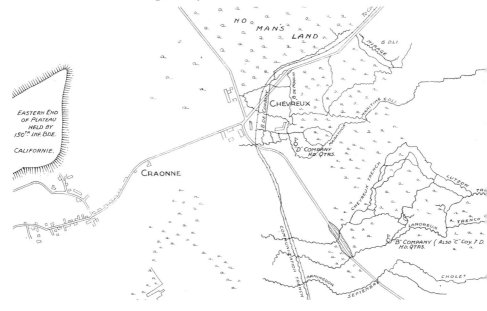

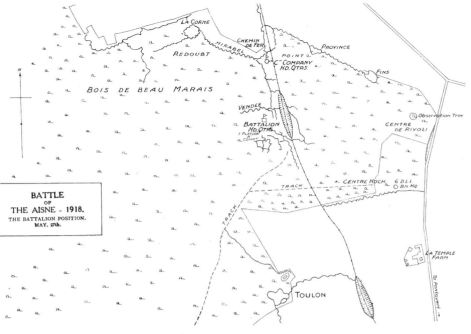

Redoubt line held by C Coy 8/DLI.

heels of the barrage, overpowered the defenders in short time and many were taken prisoner.

At 5 am a stand was made by C Company under Captain Bennett Williams, reinforced by forty machine gunners and a number of men from 7/DLI, the pioneer battalion of the brigade. These men held out for an hour along the embankment of the railway near to the Ouvrage du Chemin de Fer. Here machine and Lewis guns found excellent targets amongst the large numbers of German infantry attempting to pass through the wire. This party was eventually overwhelmed. Subdued by concentrated shellfire, only three or four managed to escape.

The battle continued in the Bois de Beaumarais, characterised by a number of isolated small scale engagements, where confusion reigned. German forces appeared in the rear and the various mixed units of men fighting independently of each other were gradually mopped up. One last stand was made to the north of the Aisne at 8 am by the acting CO of 8/DLI, Major George Gould, together with Lieutenant Colonel Arthur Birchall (7/DLI) and a party of survivors from both of these battalions.

Lieutenant Colonel P Kirkup, CO 8/DLI.

However, as in many of the actions fought by British soldiers that day, the flanks were turned and the remnants of this group were forced to retreat over the Aisne by way of the bridge at Cuiry-Les-Chaudardes. One notable casualty of this action was the second in command of 7/DLI, Major Robert Dickson, who was killed on or near the canal bridge at Maizy when leading a Lewis gun team into position. In his letter of condolence, Birchall wrote, 'I am informed that whilst holding one of the bridges over the Aisne he was shot through the chest with a rifle bullet and died immediately.' Lieutenant Colonel Kirkup, CO, 8/DLI had been ill the night before, but on the morning of the attack left the Ambulance Station and helped organize a gallant defence of Concevreux with a mixture of men from 5/NF, 5/DLI and machine gunners.

6 Durham Light Infantry

The forward position held by 6/DLI was broadly similar to that of 8/DLI on their right, except that the land was even more low lying and uniformly even in gradient. The front line was a series of outposts occupied by few troops, as Captain Hugh Lyon of X Company observed:

Lieutenant Eric A Armbrister, 8/DLI, one of sixteen officers taken prisoner in this battalion

The support line was the only line at all strongly held, and on a less healthy front we might well have had misgivings on the possible result of an attack in force. We had a shrewd idea that behind us was nothing, or practically nothing. Prisoner states that attack is coming at 4 am. Bombardment probably with gas at 1 am. Tanks may be used. Troops must fire at infantry and not at tanks. No fighting men to carry wounded. Issue extra fifty rounds per man and inspect pouches to see number is complete. All Lewis Gunners over four per team to come to Company HQ at once. Destroy all maps and important documents.

Lyon followed the order with an assessment of the men's morale:

I went round the men, who seemed cheery and confident, and saw

Chevreux in 1915, with the Chemin des Dames in the distance.

that they understood their orders. I thought their cheerfulness sufficiently marked to mention to our HQ and sent down a message: 'All serene. Men cheery as cuckoos.'

The tremendous German artillery barrage, which began at 1 am, is described in a number of reports from men of 6/DLI. Lieutenant George Roberts, writing later about his experiences of 27 May, recalled:

Captain Hugh Lyon, 6/DLI, (on the right) at Graudenz PoW camp.

Promptly at 1 am on the 27th the barrage came down, and it was such as had never been experienced by the Battalion before. Those of long war experience who lived through it stated that this was the fiercest bombardment yet known on the Western Front. The enemy flooded the whole area to a depth of about 3,000 yards with high explosive, shrapnel and gas shells. The front appeared to be one sheet of flame and gas and high explosive fell like rain.

The German tank 'Liesel' failed to negotiate British front line trenches.

Despite the fury of the bombardment, communication on this front seems to have been maintained longer than that of the 8/DLI, as messages were still being sent from the forward companies to the battalion headquarters as late as 4.50 am. One of these messages stated that an enemy tank had been reported tearing up the wire. Tanks were used in this sector by the attacking German divisions as the ground was relatively flat. Twenty tanks in four detachments were committed to battle against the 50th and 8th Divisions on a front of about six miles. All were British models, most of which had been taken at Cambrai in the previous November. Assault Tank Detachment (ATD) 14 attacked 150 Brigade. However, the threat was more apparent than real. Rainer Strasheim, in his book on *Beute-Tanks* (trophy tanks) observed:

By the time the tanks had worked their way through the initial enemy trench system, the assault infantry was off and gone. Three tanks were told to return to their assembly area. Following the advance, Wagen 117, commanded by Lieutenant Lippold...got stuck in a swampy patch of terrain and incurred damage. After

*removing valuable parts, the vehicle was abandoned and Lippold
and his crew fought on as an assault squad.*

Captain Lyon's X Company occupied the front line when the German
barrage opened up:

*I had a lance corporal on sentry duty at the head of my dugout,
who reported a great concentration of trench mortars and aerial
torpedoes on the front line, accompanied by the fire of what we
were afterwards told to be 400 guns on the front and support
trenches. I went out to him occasionally, but there was nothing I
could do until the attack came.*

At about 4.20 am Lyon decided to move his company headquarters
further forward to assess the effects of the German bombardment:

*When I came out into the open I found to my dismay and surprise
files of Germans immediately to our front and level with our line
on the right. The Germans came on leisurely, meeting with little
or no resistance. The air was full of their planes, which went
before them and swept the trenches with machine guns. A few
tanks had broken through and were now well behind us. The
defence seems to have crumpled up completely. Our own position
became almost at once untenable. A heavy machine-gun was
opened on us from our left rear, showing that the enemy would
soon be all round us, so I decided to get back while I could and
withdrew my men as fast as possible.*

Lyon was truly in awe of the tactics used by the enemy on 27 May; to
him it was a virtuoso performance, an all-arms attack without
precedent:

*I had been reckoning on the customary pause before an infantry
line can follow a barrage. But the German tactics here, well
justified by success, were to place their advance troops almost in
the skirts of their barrage, thus giving the defence no time to
recover. The intense bombardment, heavy beyond all previously
endured, had split the line into small isolated groups of sadly
shaken men, who fell an easy prey to the first German line. A
large number must have surrendered without resistance. The
speed and method of advance – nowhere did I see the slightest
confusion or hurry – filled us with a despairing admiration – I
certainly am prepared to regard the preparation and execution of
the whole attack as one of the best things an army has ever done.*

A large number of the men had only recently been seconded to the battalion and their fighting skills were not up to scratch. This was so much so that a substantial detachment from the Inland Water Transport section of the Royal Engineers, who had only been posted to 6/DLI in early May, had been at a divisional training school for most of their stay on the Aisne. 6/DLI were no different from many other battalions, in that a substantial number of the troops were boys of eighteen and nineteen. For many it was their first time in combat. Private Frank Deane's experiences were typical of many raw recruits that day. He had survived the barrage but his company had become quickly dispersed amongst the shattered trenches and dugouts. Many small, often isolated, pockets of men found themselves lacking leadership and were easily taken prisoner:

Private Frank S Deane, 6/DLI. Taken prisoner on the first day of the battle, he died in 2002 aged 103, the last British veteran of the Aisne battle.

Looking towards the front line from the Battle Zone of 6/DLI.

I can't remember a lot, everything was confused, but I recall seeing my platoon officer and he was just sat on the fire step with two men doing absolutely nothing, he just watched us go by and didn't say a word. He seemed to me to be just waiting there until the Germans caught up with him. I don't know if he actually knew what was going on or whether he was just dumbfounded. That was the only other party of the battalion that I saw that day, so you can imagine that we must have been scattered into tiny little groups.

After a couple of hours wandering along the battle front, Deane and a few others were assembled by a couple of officers into a makeshift defence, but the German infantry was now attacking in force and this small group was quickly overpowered:

The Germans came through, firing their machine guns like billy ho. We'd been lying low for protection when to the right of us a trench was spotted and we were told to get up and get to this trench. I was next to the last man, a lance corporal, but we never got anywhere near the trench before they were all around us and I was captured. Just before this a machine gun bullet crashed through the first joint of my thumb before going up my hand. My corporal friend next to me said, 'Your hand is bleeding.' I didn't know I had been hit. He took my first aid patch off my jacket and he put that on it and I would guess it stayed there for a week and was never looked at.

The sense of isolation for many men was acute. Lieutenant George Roberts recalls that all the telephone wires forward and back were cut and that it was impossible to get in touch with battalion headquarters for further instruction. Roberts's account bears witness to the ferocity of the combined arms assault of the German army in this sector:

After 4 am the shelling slackened somewhat and, while standing to, the ominous chatter of machine guns was heard through the early morning mist. Khaki figures lay all around dead or dying – and we found the enemy was right around us, we had to prepare for the end.

Shortly afterwards one of the enemy aeroplanes appeared on the scene – swooped down on to the trench where I was one of the few survivors. It came so low that we could easily discern the features of the airman and he turned his machine guns on us. A sergeant I was talking to fell dead at my feet and I went down with a bullet wound in the stomach.

Second Lieutenant WR Worrall, 5/DLI attached 151 Brigade Trench Mortar Battery, wounded and taken prisoner. Seen here in Karlsruhe PoW camp.

The reserve company of 6/DLI, Z, under Captain R Green, attempted to organise a stand near to battalion headquarters. However, due to the collapse of the front this proved impossible; enemy machine guns were firing into their position from the rear of the right flank and enemy bombers were attacking behind the left flank. A withdrawal was made down a communication trench. The commanding officer, Lieutenant Colonel Frederick Walton, along with Captain Lyon and two other officers, rallied the miscellany of troops from X and Z companies as well as elements from the reserve battalion, 5/DLI, who had moved up from the reserve area. About forty men in all were gathered together in an attempt to repel the advancing Germans. Lyon takes up the story in his diary:

> *I followed the company [of 5/DLI] down a most unhealthy communication trench, which led to a wooded hill [possibly the Butte de l'Edmond]. We could now distinguish rifle and machine gun bullets, which sounded unpleasantly close; at one point, where we had to get out of the trench to cross a road, one or two of the men were hit. By now the front of the company had reached the top of the hill to find the line already in the enemy's possession. Some were killed, some captured, and the remainder turned about and came helter-skelter down on top of us; we turned in our turn, to find the way back as bad as the way on. Men were being hit on all sides now and an aeroplane flying low added to the hail of bullets. Some of the men crept into a dugout in spite of my language and I found very few with me. When we came to the road I ran across unhurt, but of the rest who tried it nearly all were wounded or killed. I saw two Germans about 20 yards to my right and one took aim at me as I passed. Beyond this I found some cover, three or four men followed me, all but one wounded. By now I saw that the Germans were all round the hill and, looking up, I saw half a dozen of them ten yards away, shouting and raising their rifles. The wounded men were shouting at me to surrender, and indeed I saw nothing else for it. So I threw down my revolver and stood up, in a minute I was a prisoner.*

Meanwhile Colonel Walton had received a message to report to Brigade HQ (Centre d'Evreux). On arrival, the position proved to be unoccupied. Enemy machine guns were firing from the rear. Having extricated himself he managed to join up with a few men at Concevreux on the Aisne. The bridge over the river was defended until the early afternoon. This motley force comprised troops from all three battalions of 150 Brigade, as well as troops from the neighbouring 149 Brigade. Lieutenant Tom Rushworth was awarded a Military Cross for helping to organise a defence here:

> *In command of a small group of men, he held the bridgehead*

whilst under very heavy machine gun fire until the Germans outflanked his position. He withdrew his men through the village, which the Germans also entered. Holding a position in the rear of the village, he successfully patrolled the area, always under severe machine gun fire, and maintained contact with the division on his right.

5 Durham Light Infantry

5/DLI was the reserve battalion of 151 Brigade on the day of the battle. They were stationed at Chaudardes and Cuiry-Les-Chaudardes, two villages on the north bank of the Aisne. On 26 May at 7.30 pm, orders arrived from battalion headquarters stating that the companies of the battalion were to proceed at once in fighting order to Centre d'Evreux, the reserve position and also brigade headquarters. B, C and D companies were put into a series of huge dugouts near Brigade HQ and A Company into another a hundred yards away. Orders explicitly stated that the companies were to remain in these positions and not to man the trenches of the reserve position about half a mile to the north. Battalion HQ shared the same dugout as brigade HQ.

Centre d'Evreux was not a good position. Captain Veitch, staff captain of 151 Brigade, reported a number of years after the battle:

When 151 Infantry Brigade took over from the 73rd Regiment (French) on the 7th May in the Front Line, Forêt de Beau Marais, Brigade headquarters were established in P C Hoche.

After five days here we were ordered to move to Centre d'Evreux, as far as I can remember anything up to a thousand yards further to the rear. In the order was the following sentence, 'If you are attacked in your present position you will be involved in the fighting immediately and unable to control your Battalion.' On reading this General Martin said to me 'I hope to God they are not going to attack here.' Then I went with him to look at Centre d'Evreux. He asked me what I thought of it and I replied that if we were attacked no one would ever get in or out of it. He agreed. That very nearly came true. The dugout was on the forward edge of a bluff, which fell steeply down to a level clearing stretching away to P C Hoche, the position we could see. The 7th Battalion (Pioneers) had been in occupation of this dugout but were moved to make it available for Brigade headquarters.

Some of the officers serving on the Aisne.

The officer in command of C Company, Captain A B Hill, recalled the events on the eve of the attack:

About 7.20 pm on the 26th, we were sitting down to dinner when a chit arrived ordering companies to proceed at once in fighting order to Centre d'Evreux, our reserve position. On going to Battalion headquarters I found that no one had the slightest idea why this had been ordered; the impression prevailed that it was only a practice stunt! However, when I reported to Brigade headquarters this idea was quickly dispelled when the Brigade Major (Captain H J Gwyther) informed me that the Boches had been seen pouring up the line all day, and from a prisoner captured the previous evening by the 8/DLI they had learned that he was to drop his barrage at 1 am, and to attack with tanks and

Officers of the 5DLI, 1915.

*infantry at 4 am. Our reserve position was in some trenches about
half a mile to the north of Centre d'Evreux. We had not to go there
till further orders, and B, C and D Companies were put in a huge
dug-out near Brigade headquarters, and A Company into another
a hundred yards away.*

Throughout the German preliminary bombardment the men of 5/DLI
were confined to their underground quarters. At 6.30 am orders arrived
calling for C and D companies to move forward to man the trenches of
the Battle Zone to the north. However, due to the severe disruption of
the communication system in the region of Centre d'Evreux, the orders
arrived too late. The two forward companies were advancing into
positions that had already been overrun by German troops. Major A L
Raimes noted in his history of the battalion:

*As they groped their way along the communication trenches with
their respirators on they found themselves in close contact with
the enemy. There was no time to get into proper battle formation.
Officers gathered their men together as best they could, and put
them into positions where they could use their rifles and Lewis
guns. The confusion was great, and, surrounded as they were by
thick woods that obscured their view of other parts of the
battlefield, it was impossible for them to know what had
happened. It was obvious, however, that a fearful disaster had
occurred and the officers tried to get their men clear of the woods
and back to the Aisne bridges, while taking advantage of any
opportunities of holding up the enemy.*

Meanwhile the remaining two companies, A and B, were waiting to
advance but, according to Captain Veitch, the runner with orders from
Brigade Headquarters failed to reach the dugouts of 5/DLI, even
though this was less than a hundred yards distant. As a result these two
companies were, as the Brigade Headquarters diary relates:
'Surrounded and captured before they could leave their shelters. No
news of them is to hand.'

In a similar manner to other battalions, men from
5/DLI fought on in isolated groups, retreating
towards the Aisne bridges. During the day nine of
the officers were killed and five wounded, a very
high percentage even for 27 May, given that most of
these casualties came from the two companies that
had attempted to reach the fortifications of the Battle
Zone. Nevertheless, some detachments were able

Captain Norman Hessler,
KiA whilst organising a
stand north of Centre
d'Evreux.

65

Captain W Moscrop and brother officers of 5/DLI. He is second from the right.

to fight staunch rearguard actions. Captain Norman Hessler (commanding A company), one of two brothers of Norwegian descent who fought in the battalion (his brother was killed during the March offensive), organised a defence in a clearing north west of Pontavert. This group held up the enemy for a considerable period of time before Hessler was killed whilst firing a Lewis gun. The remnants of the group fell back to the Aisne and joined with other mixed bands of men from the 50th and 8th Divisions in attempting to stem the enemy assault over the canal and river. Here the battalion adjutant, Captain William Moscrop, attempted to organise a hasty defence of a bridge near Maizy. He was confirmed as killed when his and other graves were discovered in 1919 – the location indicating that he and his group of men died fighting whilst covering the bridge at the south end of Maizy. Captain Moscrop's body was then reburied in Vendresse British Cemetery.

Captain Veitch provides a vivid account of the confusion that ensued in the vicinity of the Aisne during the late morning of 27 May:

The first wave of German shock troops make for the bridge at Pont-Arcy.

I recrossed the Aisne Canal and made my way along its north bank towards Chaudardes and passed the end of a further bridge over the canal at the western end of Concevreux where men of various battalions were taking up defensive positions. When I reached the bridge over the river Aisne leading into Chaudardes I found a sapper NCO lying at the south end of the bridge busy with fuses for its demolition. Whilst there a field kitchen of the 5th Battalion DLI came at full gallop out of Chaudardes, over the bridge and got away, and as it passed me on the bridge end I saw a 5th DLI officer who was wounded lying on it. We were being fired on at the bridge and so I realised there was no getting to Beaurieux [50th Division Headquarters] that way and after a while made my way back down a ditch to Concevreux, crossed the bridge and followed the canal south bank in the direction of Maizy. Perhaps two hundred yards along the road at the end of the third bridge I found the 6th Battalion Headquarters DLI established. Colonel Walton told me of the death of General Martin [GOC 151 Brigade]. I did not know until then, for when we left Centre d'Evreux we came out of the dugout by a different entrance and did not see him lying there.

The War Diary relates the experiences of one detachment of the battalion as it fell back to the Aisne:

> *This detachment withdrew and held a position in the clearing north-west of Pontavert, and held up the enemy for a considerable time. Ammunition was very short. The enemy were found to be round both flanks, and a withdrawal was made to a line held by a portion of the 25th Division. The enemy had by this time crossed the Aisne higher up, and it was plain that the position then held was likely to be turned. It was decided to withdraw to Chaudardes, but a reconnaissance ascertained that the enemy were between them and the village so the proposed movement was impossible. Nearly all this detachment was cut off, a few escaping over the Aisne before the bridge was blown.*

Leutnant Ammer's company of the Infantry Regiment 158 attacked near Pontavert during the morning of 27 May. He recalled:

> *Having passed the Viller Berg* [Bois des Buttes] *by the flank, my company and I raced for Pontavert, that was two kilometres in the distance and reached it around 9.15 am. The way to Pontavert was a manhunt. We killed a lot of the British who fled and didn't take cover or surrender quickly enough. We approached the village by a trench along the main road and entered a food depot filled with the finest stuff. Suddenly three British appeared, coming out of a tiny cabin, two of them firing Lewis guns. I and my men took cover and started firing with our rifles. One man fell down, being hit in the shoulder another shot through the head and the final one hit in the chest. This last soldier, a big fellow, fired at us again, but was finally killed by a shot to the head. In Pontavert I looked over a wall of a farmhouse and was able to see the bridge over the canal, which suddenly exploded right in front of me. Too bad, I thought. Fleeing British soldiers ran from behind us and passed by to reach the canal. Lots of them were killed by rifle fire that came from 'their' side of the front. In the beginning we took three prisoners, but they tried to escape so we shot them down.*

68

**Corporal JS Thornley,
5/DLI, KiA 27 May.**

A number of battalion war diaries and regimental histories of the units involved in the fighting on the first day of the Aisne battle talk of them being reduced to a cadre or, more poignantly, 'annihilated'; of these, 5/DLI perhaps warrants this dubious accolade the most. The casualties of the battalion on 27 May were twenty four officers and about 650 men. Of the officers, ten were killed, five wounded and nine taken prisoner. Of the other ranks, fifty-three were killed and 151 were wounded and brought back across the Aisne to safety. 446 were taken prisoner, but this includes a large number of wounded who had to be left. In comparison with other battalions of 151 Brigade, the number of officers killed or wounded in 6/DLI and 8/DLI was substantially lower, six and five respectively. Larger numbers of officers were taken prisoner in these battalions, some sixteen in the case of 6/DLI and seventeen in 8/DLI. As far as other ranks are concerned, twenty-six men from 6/DLI were killed and thirty-three from 8/DLI. The reasons why 5/DLI suffered proportionally higher casualties than the other two battalions of the brigade is explained by

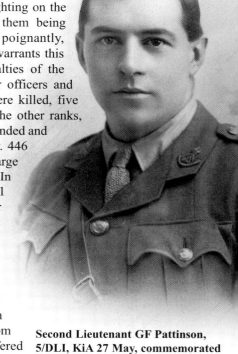

Second Lieutenant GF Pattinson, 5/DLI, KiA 27 May, commemorated on the Soissons Memorial.

the fact that, being in reserve, they were called up to fortify the Battle Zone, which had already been overrun by the enemy. As a result, many men from the battalion were fighting in the open and not from entrenched positions.

The rate of attrition endured by 5/DLI can also be compared with other actions that the battalion was involved in during the Great War. No action prior to 1918 comes close in terms of casualties, the next highest being the Battle of Arras between 21 to 24 April 1917, when 263 men were killed, wounded or taken prisoner. During the German offensives of 1918, the battalion suffered 334 casualties on the Somme (in twelve days of action) and 423 on the Lys (five days). In the first three days of the Battle of the Aisne, 27 to 29 May, the battalion lost 650 men, the vast majority on the first day. This rate of loss easily equates to the high casualty rates of infantry battalions involved in other days of disaster for the British army in the Great War, namely 1 July 1916 and 21 March 1918.

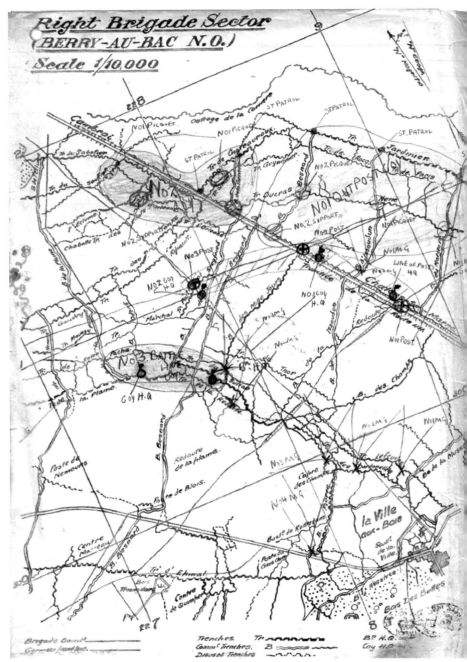

149 Brigade sector held by 6/NF, outpost line and 4/NF, battle zone.

149 Brigade

An authoritative and detailed account of the disposition and performance of 149 Brigade in the Battle of the Aisne was written by its commander, Brigadier General Edward Riddell, in October 1918. His analysis of the tactical problems of the sector occupied by the 50th Division was evident when, like many of his fellow commanders, he expressed deep concern over the French insistence on a rigid defence north of the Aisne. Like other divisional and brigade commanders, he would have preferred to have held on to this ground merely as a line of outposts, using the south bank of the Aisne as the main line of resistance.

Although critical of the French High Command, Riddell was also understanding. He realised the sacrifice the French had made the previous year in wresting the control of the Chemin des Dames from the enemy; although giving up the higher ground would have been sensible from a military point of view, it was to all intents and purpose a political impossibility. In these circumstances Riddell's approach was fatalistically pragmatic:

> During our tour in the line, every conceivable plan of attack by the Bosch was considered and dispositions made to meet it; but a man and a gun can be in only one place at a time; and we had so few men and guns!

149 Brigade held the front line as a series of outposts, with the main line of resistance some 1,500 yards further back. 151 Brigade, to the left, and 23 Brigade of the 8th Division to the right had adopted the same system, except the outposts or 'picquets' were smaller and more numerous. This, according to Riddell, made the line weaker as it was much harder to control by battalion headquarters. Another more serious difference concerned the defensive positions of the area south of the Battle Zone. 149 Brigade had, during their brief occupation of the trench system, developed a formidable barrier in the form of four fortified redoubts between 500 and 700 yards behind the Battle Zone. Each of these redoubts was held by one company of the support battalion as well as having four machine gun and two heavy mortar teams. These weapons were well placed and could provide direct fire over the Battle Zone if required. Additionally, two anti-tank guns were placed behind the line of the redoubts on slightly rising ground, covered in brushwood camouflage. As Riddell pointed out; 'The units on my right and left had no strong line to correspond to this reserve battle line, although they did have machine guns posts.'

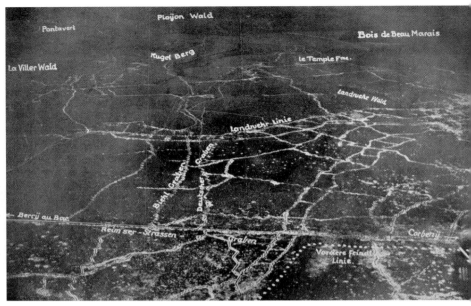

German aerial photograph of 149 Brigade's sector.

At 6 pm on 26 May, in a meeting between Riddell and Major General Henry Jackson, GOC the 50th Division, it was determined that 149 Brigade should:

> *fight it out to a finish on our Battle line. No outside help could reach us in time. Brigades were to bring their reserve battalion to the North bank of the Aisne and use it for counter-attack. The arrival of French Divisions in time would depend entirely on our ability to hold the Bosch* (sic) *North of the Aisne.*

Riddell had reservations about this method of defence:

> *We know from experience in this war that an attack in force will invariably over-run a weakly held position to a depth of two to three miles, if well supported by artillery. In spite of this accepted principle, we had no garrisoned defensive zone South of the Aisne.*

Each division in the front line of IX Corps had been given the option of calling on a brigade of the 25th Division (the reserve division) if necessity arose; but Riddell was concerned that if reserve brigades were called upon in such an event there would be no prepared reserve defensive position to fall back on. Divisional commanders had made their thoughts known to higher authority concerning the use of reserve formations in battle but, for the military and political reasons stated in

German assault troops, who spearheaded the attack 27 May. Note pouches for grenades.

a previous chapter, the French were committed to fighting north of the Aisne. Riddell, along with his fellow senior officers, favoured the use of a strongly defended Rear Zone south of the Aisne river and canal.

As the German advance continued it was not long before the headquarters of both 151 and 149 Brigades became the front line. Just after 6 am Riddell had left his quarters and joined Brigadier General Martin with a view to organising a last ditch attempt at holding Centre d'Evreux with two companies of the 5/NF. Martin informed Riddell of the situation with regard to the collapse of his brigade front to the north and west. From this Riddell deduced that his brigade was practically surrounded, but there was a chance of saving some of it if the better trenches, with an equally improved field of fire, at Centre d'Evreux could be effectively utilised by his remaining troops. Both brigadiers were now in the thick of the battle:

When a sentry told us that fighting was going on in the woods about us, I knew that the battle for Centre d'Evreux had commenced, and that we should have to take it instead of holding it. It was 'all hands to the pumps' now. Martin still had thirty odd men and staff about him. We ordered everybody to turn out, and climbed out of the dug-out to join the 5th N F. It was quite clear, with a bright sun. Shells were bursting all about us and machine gun bullets flipped the leaves and smacked into the trees. We could hear the Lewis gun of the platoon of the 5/DLI 'rat tatting' away behind us, showing that we were holding on, but to the North of me I caught sight of a few Bosches close to hand in the bushes. Martin and I, with Leathheart of the gunners, ran on

Wagen107, one of four tanks that accompanied 158 IR on its attack on 149 Brigade. This was the only tank to survive the action. (Rainier Strasheim)

towards the 5th N F. We had only gone a few yards when a shell burst on our left. I felt a terrific blow in the face, and saw Martin roll over. I went to him. He was quite dead. I walked on half dazed, with a great hole in my face into which I could put my hand, but I did not feel much pain. The Bosch was now firing on us with rifle and machine gun from close at hand to the East as we crossed the open. Over my left shoulder I could see our men and Bosches mixed together. When I reached the headquarters of the 5th N F I found only one platoon; the rest had gone forward. The German rifle fire died down and the machine guns ceased fire. The 5th N F must have retaken Centre d'Evreux. I had not been too late after all.

Riddell and Martin could not have been closer to the action on the morning of 27 May. Despite being badly wounded, Riddell continued to give orders and helped to rally a makeshift defence of the Aisne and its bridges out of stragglers of the 50th Division, before he was hurried away in a field ambulance.

Trench map of the battle zone held by 4/NF.

4 Northumberland Fusiliers

The intelligence officer of 149 Brigade, Captain Eric Bell MC, witnessed the opening bombardment of the German artillery on his brigade front, from where the 4/NF were positioned. Almost twenty years later he wrote:

Just before midnight I went forward to an OP [Observation Post] *about 100 yards in front of Brigade HQ. I stood with my watch in hand, waiting for the seconds to reach midnight; up to that moment our guns were firing furiously but there was no response from the German lines. On the stroke of midnight the whole horizon, as far as one could see, behind the German lines lit up as though with an enormous flash of lightning; it was the most thrilling and dramatic sight I saw in the course of 18 months trench experience, and the bombardment which followed was sustained at a heavier rate than any other which I experienced. The only thing I recall to equal it was in April 1916 in front of the Petit Bois at Wyschaete.*

A large number of mixed H E and gas shells were used, so that in a short time it was necessary to use masks outside gas proof dugouts; as usual at this time of the year there was a certain amount of early morning mist; the heavy shell bursts in the sandy soil caused much dust and these three conditions together brought about a spate of fog, and made observation very bad. This applied especially to the Buttes on our right, which were enshrouded almost completely in a dusty smoke.

Bell also witnessed the initial German infantry attack on the positions held by 149 Brigade:

The attack came at 4 am [other reports from 149 Brigade's front suggest 3 am] *and was directed principally on the front line east of the Laon-Rheims road until these* [positions] *were overcome. The posts put up the best resistance they could, but I understand that the divisional front was attacked by five and a half divisions, and they were surrounded in the bad light, and dealt with at leisure. Conditions could not have been better for the German methods of infiltration: the front was held thinly, with many gaps, the numerous unoccupied old trenches gave good cover to advancing parties, and the smoke and dust hid them till they were close to the posts and prevented the latter from seeing what was passing between them. As soon as the Laon-Rheims road was secured, the advance was continued and arrived in a short time in front of the battle position. This was crossed about 7 am, although resistance continued in the posts for several hours afterwards.*

4/NF occupied the front line trenches of the Brigade position on the morning of 24 May, relieving 5/NF. Two companies occupied the outposts and picquet lines (effectively the old front line), another company manned a line of posts and trenches along the Route 44 Reims-Laon road, with a further company and battalion headquarters lodged in the most northerly redoubt of the Battle Zone, Trench de la Plaine. News was received of the impending German attack at 7.30 pm on 26 May and all the necessary defensive measures were taken by the battalion. This involved the picquet line falling back to the trenches along Route 44, leaving only sentry groups to watch the area of outposts. Orders were received from Brigade HQ that as soon as the attack commenced, artillery and stokes mortar fire was to pepper the outpost line and wire entanglements of No Man's Land, with the sentry groups falling back as soon as they had fired the SOS on seeing the enemy.

The entry in the War Diary of 4/NF for the attack that commenced at 1 pm on 27 May is remarkably detailed in comparison with other war diaries that deal with the events of that day:

The enemy put down an extraordinarily intensive barrage on the whole of the Forward Area, composed of H E and gas mixed. All troops standing to in their Battle positions and many casualties were caused through the shelling. At 3.45 am enemy attacked along the whole line on the battalion front, they apparently came from behind the Ouvrage de la Carrière in a south-easterly direction almost parallel to Route 44. The survivors of the outpost company withdrew to the line of posts where Lewis Gun and rifle fire broke up the attack and drove back the enemy

One of the main reasons for the enemy's lack of immediate penetration in this area of the front line was down to the careful preparation that had been made by 149 Brigade. The withdrawal from the outpost and picquet line and the bombardment of the old front line positions by the divisional artillery caused the German troops considerable problems. The advanced positions occupied by 4/NF were eventually enveloped by German troops from both flanks; a direct attack had been ruled out due to the stiff resistance of those companies of fusiliers occupying the line of posts along Route 44. The method of defence in depth carried out by well drilled troops worked well in this sector; many men survived the preliminary bombardment here, due to their early withdrawal from the outpost line; other battalions were not so timely in removing troops from such exposed positions.

The stout resistance of the men holding the positions along the main road was eventually overcome at 4 am, the enemy having had to attack three times in this area. The final assault, which included the use of four tanks, eventually succeeded in pushing the forward companies of the Northumberland back to the Battle Zone. Many men of the left forward company were either killed or taken prisoner as they withdrew, as the enemy had managed to turn the flank from the right and the men of this company found the enemy already in their rear.

It was not long after this that the Battle Zone was attacked. The German tanks that had penetrated the line to the north continued their advance, forcing Lieutenant Colonel Bertrand Gibson, CO of 4/NF, to move his battalion headquarters back to the line of redoubts at Centre Marceau. Again, the main line of assault came from the right flank, in the direction of La Ville-aux-Bois, the area occupied by the 8th Division, and troops of both 4/NF and 6/NF, the support battalion, found the enemy attacking from the rear. Resistance in the Battle Zone was overcome by 4.45 am.

Captain JV Gregory, Adjutant 4/NF, wounded in three places and later carried to hospital.

Telephone communication was established at Centre Marceau between Gibson and Brigade HQ. At 5 am Gibson informed Riddell that he was still holding on to the line of redoubts with forty men, but the situation was looking fairly grim. Riddell recalled the conversation:

> *I told him to hold out to the last and that I would order a company of the 5/NF in reserve to retake Temple Farm and help his left. I can hear his brave, firm voice now as he said: 'Very good, sir, Good-bye.' I suppose he knew that there was no chance. The man on the spot, if he is a good man, always knows best. I heard afterwards that he was shot through the head while cheering on his men in a final effort. A splendid death for a splendid man.*

German Attack on the Butte de L'Edmond.

Pontavert   Butte de L'Edmond   Chemin des Dames

4th North. Fusiliers   Redoubt Line

5th North. Fusiliers

German Advance

Bois des Buttes

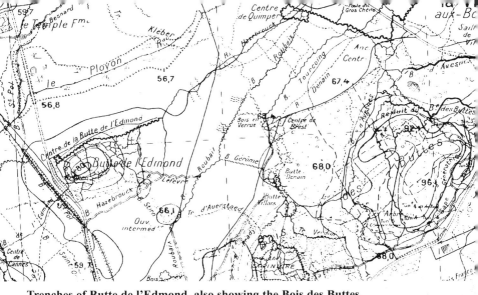

Trenches of Butte de l'Edmond, also showing the Bois des Buttes.

By 5.30 am the enemy had taken the redoubt line again from the right and rear. Gibson and a handful of men fell back to Butte de l'Edmond, where they joined a party of the divisional Machine Gun Battalion and made a further stand. Here Gibson was killed. A terse entry – like many other entries for 27 May – in the War Diary states: 'From this time the 4/NF ceased to exist as a fighting unit'.

Reverend Wilfrid Callin CF wrote of this heroic stand by the 4/NF in his memoir, *When the Lantern of Hope Burned Low*:

> *The whole line was deluged with shells, and the front trenches especially must have been reduced to a pulverised mass. For two hours and a half this continued; then lifted further on as the infantry and tanks attacked at 3.30 am. Then ensued a fight that had epic qualities. Standing in the ruins of their defences, the Northumberlands awaited the onslaught - waited and met it with rifle and Lewis gun fire until the grey hordes broke and stayed their course, tanks and men alike. Another battalion came to their help,* [most likely the 5/NF] *and the wood in front of Pontavert became a perfect hell. Draw a line from the front of that wood eastwards to the Bois des Buttes and you have roughly the line on which the Fourth fought its last battle as a battalion. The enemy came on in*

Rev. R Wilfrid Callin, recorded the exploits of the 4/NF in a post war memoir.

79

great force diagonally from the right, between Ronteux and the line running Ville-aux-Bois / Bois des Buttes, so getting in behind the battalion and working towards Craonne. Thus they were almost completely cut off. Out of the mêlée only a few emerged. Marshall came down gassed and, after a certain rest and treatment at Concevreux, returned to the fight with Major Robb's party, Napier (barely recovered from his wound) came down badly gassed and had to be sent to hospital. Captain Gregory, the Adjutant, was wounded and reported to have been left in the marshes, but by the almost super human courage of two of our men, Hunter and Coghlan, was carried out and eventually reached hospital, wounded in three places. Captain Benson, of the Trench Mortar Battery, having made his way to the forefront of the fight, led an attack on a German tank, but was killed in the effort. Colonel Gibson fell, shot through the head as he was directing the last defences. With the enemy on every side, the River and Canal both behind them, the survivors, on the exhaustion of ammunition, were taken prisoner.

Major J Ridley Robb, second in command, 4/NF, ordered a makeshift defence of the bridges over the Aisne.

By 9 am most of the remnants of 149 Brigade had fallen back in the direction of the Aisne river and canal between Chaudardes and Concevreux (which became the new position of Brigade HQ). The Brigade Major, H W Jackson, along with Major Ridley Robb, of 4/NF, organised a hasty defence. Captain Jackson, in a letter to Riddell, described the last ditch attempt to guard the bridges over the Aisne - the details providing an evocative picture of an army in retreat:

Well, you will remember the perfect stream of men coming along the canal bank from the direction of Pontavert. I stopped these men at the bridge - there were no more than 2% of NCOs and no officers. I suppose I collected some 200 in due course - formed them up in two ranks and told them off into sections and platoons on the canal bank. There were men of the 8th Division,

Lance Corporal M O'Brien, 4/NF, awarded a Croix de Guerre with gold star, for his command of a Lewis gun Section near the Aisne river.

149th and 151st Brigades and other details. I explained the situation to all the men as best I could, formed four composite platoons and placed them in position. My greatest difficulty was having no officers and I remember having to go to the extremity of drawing my revolver on two men who tried to go back. The danger came from the right flank as the Boche had taken Pontavert, gained the crossings there over the river and canal and was working south-west on the south side of the canal, the time being 9.30 am.

Major Robb (4th N.F.) came up about that time. I handed over to him and said I would go along to the left, find out what was happening, find Major Tweedy (Commander 4th N.F.) and establish a brigade headquarters in Concevreux. Just as I was going off, a major of the Worcesters came along the canal bank in a car! Apparently a battalion of the Worcesters – 25th Division – was coming up to help us. We discussed the situation to the accompaniment of a few 'pings' from a Boche sniper's rifle. I said I thought two companies should counter-attack along the southern bank of the canal with the blowing up of Pontavert bridge (about 1,200 yards away) as their objective, as I was convinced that only a few Boche had crossed the canal up to that time, but it was certain that the 8th Division (who I think were responsible) – had failed to blow up the bridge. Also touch had to be gained with the 8th Division. The Worcesters did eventually go up to our right flank but were too late to achieve anything in the form of a counter attack.

Major Robb held the position along the Aisne canal until 1 pm when a withdrawal took place to conform to a line held by the 3rd Worcestershire Regiment. Robb was awarded the Chevalier de la Légion d'Honneur for his actions defending the bridge near Chaudardes that day, and two other officers of 4/NF, Lieutenant J M Goodbody and Second Lieutenant A Marshall, won MCs for helping to rally the troops on the Aisne canal bank.

6 Northumberland Fusiliers

The 6/NF held a line of redoubts roughly 500 yards behind the battle line. The four redoubts: Bastion de Rotterdam, Centre de Quimper, Poste de Blois and Centre Marceau, were held by two companies of the battalion, with four machine guns and two heavy trench mortars in emplacements that could fire over the battle line. The remaining companies were in reserve in trenches and dug outs next to Lieutenant Colonel Temperley's battalion HQ at P C Kleber. Like the positions of other front line battalions, the trenches and underground shelters of 6/NF were also pulverised by the German preliminary bombardment. By 5 am the battle line had been broken on the front of 149 Brigade, and German stormtroop units and tanks were already advancing on Centre Marceau, which was now held by mixed units of the 4th and 6th battalions. By 5.30 am Temperley had ordered a counter attack with his reserve company, which managed to push the enemy out of Bastion de Rotterdam, but Quimper had fallen. Nevertheless, the advanced units of the German infantry managed to work around the redoubts, which were taken from the rear. A large number of men from 6/NF were taken prisoner, especially officers, some seventeen in all, including Temperley.

Captain Joseph Garrard, a company commander in 6/NF, wrote to General Edmonds of his experiences in the battle in 1935, commenting on a draft copy of the Official History he had received. He had served with the battalion since 1915 and was concerned that the role of the 50th Division in May 1918 should be accurately represented: 'I am pleased to note the mention in the draft of tired British divisions and also of imperfectly trained recruits and feel some satisfaction that these statements will be put on record.'

Despite expressing his high regard for the generals and battalion commanders under whom he served, he was concerned about the lack of preparations that had been made in his sector prior to the attack:

> *There appeared generally a distinct lack of co-operation between infantry and Machine Gun Corps. They were miles apart metaphorically as far as operations were concerned and the latter seemed to be satisfied if their crews knew their SOS lines, which from my point of view seemed to be hopeless and useless, I being on the spot as it were.*
>
> *At the commencement of the German attack the M.G.C. (two teams) had totally expended their ammunition and were useless to me; I chased them back to their next positions, which they did not know.*

He was also anxious that measures had not been taken to counter the four German tanks that attacked in his sector, as no armour piercing ammunition had been issued to either the infantry or the machine gunners; consequently the tanks came on unmolested.

Garrard's concluding, battle weary, assessment was that,

Major JG Leathart MC (centre), 6/NF, awarded MC for conspicuous devotion to duty over eight days during the Aisne battle.

The morale of the German troops was not very great even with the bolstering up that their victories in March and April might have given them and if the British troops had only been in better condition and a little more set a different tale would have been told. It was a very unsatisfactory business, rotten in fact, yet taking everything into account no faults could be found anywhere and everyone did one's best, poor as it was.

Garrard served on the Western Front with the 50th Division since 'its baptism at St Julian in 1915', and had served in almost every 'show' that they had fought. In this context his view remains bleak but perhaps understandable.

Private HV Allan, 5/NF, probably died from wounds received on the first day of the battle and is buried in Marfaux British Cemetery

5 Northumberland Fusiliers

5/NF were the reserve battalion of 149 Brigade on 27 May. They were based at Concevreux, south of the Aisne, under the command of Major Ivan Tweedy. In terms of numbers the battalion was in a relatively healthy position, almost brought up to full strength on 30 April by the addition of a new draft and now with a complement of thirty-seven officers and 936 other ranks. Despite the apparent numerical strength of the unit, many of the men were young recruits and a number of the officers were drafted in from Irish regiments. It would take a while before unit cohesion could be fostered. The reminiscences of Private Percy Williams illustrate these difficulties. He was one of the young recruits recently drafted into the battalion and saw action for the first time on the Aisne.

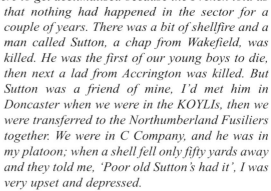

Private Percy Williams 5/NF, only 18 when made a PoW, died in 1999 aged 100.

We were sent into a quiet sector, which we had taken over from the French near Reims, a place called Fismes. We were just manning the lines, we didn't do anything, we thought we were just there to get acclimatised because the French told us that nothing had happened in the sector for a couple of years. There was a bit of shellfire and a man called Sutton, a chap from Wakefield, was killed. He was the first of our young boys to die, then next a lad from Accrington was killed. But Sutton was a friend of mine, I'd met him in Doncaster when we were in the KOYLIs, then we were transferred to the Northumberland Fusiliers together. We were in C Company, and he was in my platoon; when a shell fell only fifty yards away and they told me, 'Poor old Sutton's had it', I was very upset and depressed.

At 1 am on the morning of 27 May, when the German bombardment opened up, despite being in reserve, the trenches of 5/NF had also been targeted. Although not as devastating as the shelling of the front line positions, confusion reigned:

We did not know what was happening, not fifty yards on either side of us. There were no

Private Tom Williams, 5/NF, taken prisoner at Pontavert.

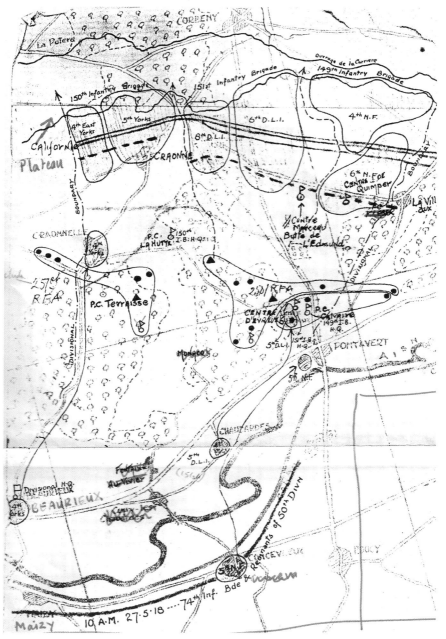

50th Division area sketch map.

communications. Then Corporal Collins came along. He was panicking, he'd seen tanks, he said that the Germans had broken through, and we were surrounded. As I stumbled from the trench I dropped my rifle, it was panic, the noise was terrible. I was weighed down by my pack, by fifty rounds of ammunition strapped around me, by my entrenching tool, the earth was blown up all around and I couldn't see.

At 2.40 am the battalion was ordered by brigade to move up to a position south east of Beaurepaire woods. They were once again heavily shelled as they moved northwards and

German officers inspect British prisoners at Craonne.

reached their destination at 4 am, in open ground adjacent to the village of Pontavert. This was a fatal mistake, one endured by most of the reserve battalions of IX Corps that were moved northwards on the morning of the attack. Riddell, one of the more enlightened commanding officers with regard to the positioning of his units on the Aisne - as demonstrated above - was as guilty as other commanders in committing his reserve battalion too hastily into the battle. In many cases this was an ad hoc response to the collapse of front line positions, an attempt to shore up second line defences threatened by the German onslaught. However, in many instances the enemy had already taken these defences before the reserve battalion could be moved into position. The more sensible alternative would have been to man the banks of the Aisne river and canal and to wait for the arrival of the units of the 25th Division - the reserve division - that were already moving towards the river from the south. Of course, it is easy to make this criticism with the benefit of hindsight, but Riddell was aware of the

Lieutenant Oliver Young, 5/NF, won an MC for helping to organise the defence of the bridge at Concevreux. (Colin Young)

value of the Aisne as a defensive position of some magnitude and mentioned this in his post battle report:

> *Most undoubtedly, the position south of the Aisne was infinitely stronger than that which we held north of the river, and should have been regarded as our main line of resistance…and considered our positions north of the river in the light of outposts.*

Lieutenant Oliver Young, MC citation.

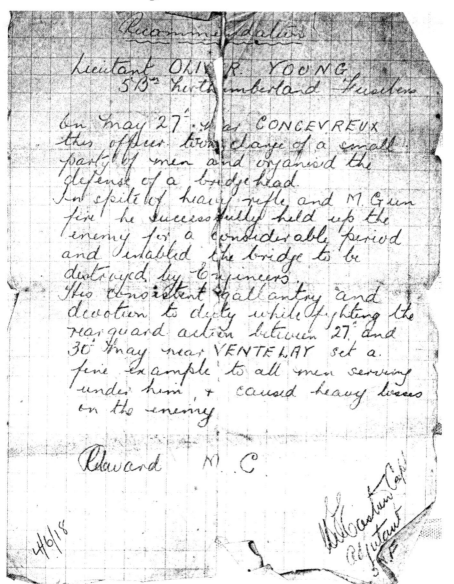

Sergeant Henry T Robson conducts 5/NF bayonet practice at Strensall barracks, York.

> *I wish we had done so – but we were under orders of the French Army and needs must obey.*

Nevertheless, Riddell was constrained by the defensive system adopted by the British, which called for the use of reserve formations in a counter attacking role, and without doubt this would have been expected in battle circumstances as far as his superiors were concerned.

5/NF were fed piecemeal into the battle as the front line and battle zone crumbled under the weight of the German advance. Riddell ordered C and D Companies to occupy the intermediate line between Butte de l'Edmond and Bois des Buttes at 5.15 am, under the command of Colonel Temperley, the CO of 6/NF. However, the message did not

Sergeant Henry T Robson (right) with his father and two brothers. All three brothers were sergeants with the NF.

arrive until after 6 am, by which time the Butte de l'Edmond had fallen to the enemy. As the two companies moved north they came under an intense barrage and C Company was unable to occupy the Butte de l'Edmond-Bois des Buttes line due to heavy machine gun fire. A stand was made by the remnants of both companies in trenches to the south of the Butte de l'Edmond:

> *Here followed a stiff fight in which the advantage was with the 5/NF, for they were able to shoot from the trench and had accounted for most of the Bosches before they had time to take cover.*

It was not long before the flank was turned and enemy troops advancing from the Bois des Buttes were soon behind trenches occupied by 5/NF. Many were taken prisoner, but a few, under the command of Major Leatheart (6/NF), managed to fight their way back to join the troops holding the Aisne.

Second Lieutenant S Weaterton, 5/NF, taken prisoner on 27 May.

Meanwhile A and B Companies, commanded by Major Tweedy, were ordered by Riddell to advance to the trenches adjacent to Brigade HQ at Centre d'Evreux and block the German advance on Pontavert. This proved impossible, as the enemy were already in the woods to the north. As related above, Riddell was by now badly wounded and at this

To the victors the spoils. German soldiers and the aftermath of battle.

50th Division Signal Company RE. The officer seated in the front row is Captain AE Odell, MC and Bar, who narrowly escaped imprisonment.

point Major Tweedy took over as officer commanding what was left of 149 Brigade. The remaining troops of 5/NF were ordered to fall back towards the Aisne at Chaudardes. Here they joined other troops of 149 and 151 Brigades occupying the bridges along the Aisne canal and river.

Sapper Bob Edward's photograph. On the back he wrote, 'View from the British front line just before the German push of May 27th 1918 Chemin des Dames France'.

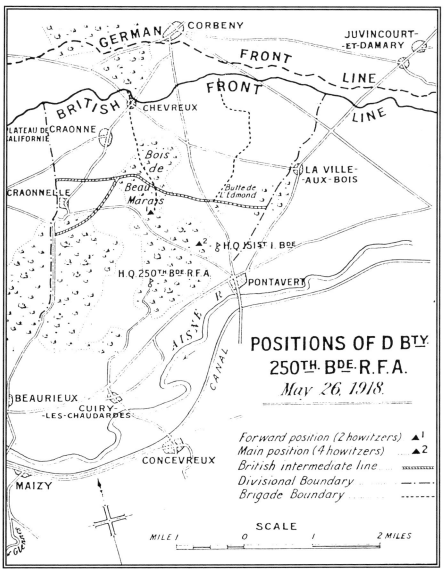

POSITIONS OF D B^{TY}·
250TH· B^{DE}·R.F.A.
May 26, 1918.

Forward position (2 howitzers) ▲¹
Main position (4 howitzers) ....▲²
British intermediate line .... ▭▭▭
Divisional Boundary .... —·—
Brigade Boundary .... ------

SCALE
MILE 1   0   1   2 MILES

D Battery, CCL Brigade RFA position on 26 May.

91

50th Division Artillery

The artillery of the 50th Division comprised two brigades, the CCL (I Northumbrian) and the CCLI (II Northumbrian). Both brigades arrived on the Aisne front in early May. The CCL Brigade's role was to cover the infantry of 149 and 150 Brigade, and was stationed north west of Pontavert in a large wood, the Bois de Beaumarais. The wood was so thick that one of the first jobs of the gun crews was to cut down trees for several hundreds of yards in front of their positions. Despite this, the operating positions were some of the best that the brigade had encountered on the Western Front, as Major F 'Archie' Shiel remembered:

> *The positions were most comfortable, especially A Battery's, with good, deep dug-outs for officers and men. The wood was full of violets, lilies of the valley...Wagon-lines were at Glennes* [south of the Aisne] *and there, too, everything was bon, billets and horse standings being of the best...The OPs were under the Craonne plateau. Literally under, for to reach them one went underground through long passages until one arrived at a door marked with the number of the Battery or position to which it belonged. These doors led to rooms from which one looked out across the country through a slit cut in the hillside. They were the most perfect OPs we had ever seen. We patted ourselves on the back and said: 'This is where war is waged by perfect gents, the place we have long been seeking'.*

Nevertheless, Shiel still had misgivings:

Officers 1st Northumbrian Brigade (CCL) RFA. Major F Shiel (fourth from right, sitting).

Here was this crack French division sent off to prepare for a great enemy attack which had not come off, and they had for the first time in their lives, I believe, been doing two or three months trench warfare. Here were we, then, a twice broken division, made up this time with boys under eighteen to relieve them, and on either side was a similar division. Can you wonder that my betting book was opened at six to four on an attack?

The CCLI Brigade RFA occupied the left sector of the front covering 151 Brigade. The battery positions were well built and well situated for offensive warfare, but not very well sited for defensive operations. B and C batteries were south west of Craonnelle, on high ground, with the gun pits running parallel to the Chemin des Dames, which was roughly a mile to the north. A and B batteries and headquarters were in a wood, Bois Vallet.

Despite the illusion of tranquillity, news reached CCLI Brigade Headquarters at 8 pm on 26 May from Divisional Artillery that a heavy bombardment followed by an attack on a large scale was to take place on the Chemin des Dames ridge shortly after midnight. Orders were later received with instructions for all guns to put down a bombardment on all roads and approaches behind the enemy front line starting at 9 pm to continue until midnight. Thereafter counter-preparation and counter-battery fire was not to begin *until the first discharge of violent artillery fire.* The enemy guns did not reply during this period.

Promptly at 1 am the German artillery bombardment commenced. Lieutenant A H Witherington reported, from CCLI Brigade Headquarters:

It was only a matter of seconds before every telephone wire was out and every gas curtain was blown in and we were completely cut off from everybody. All we could do therefore was to sit on the sand, with respirators on, awaiting developments.

A 7.30 am a runner from A Battery arrived at its Brigade HQ and reported that the front line had been pushed back but Brigadier General Rees was still optimistic that the Craonne plateau could be held. No other messages were received. Just after 8 am, accordingly to Witherington:

There was a shout. It was from Burgess, [Barton's orderly], informing us that there was a Boche at the entrance to our tunnel. This news was incredible. Surely Burgess must have been mistaken - perhaps he had been shell shocked! Such a development would not have surprised us at anytime during the

93

March retreat, but not here, the quietest front we had ever experienced.

I rushed to the entrance to the tunnel and there, sure enough, Boches with bayonets fixed were peering down the tunnel. A further quick glance was all that was necessary to show that literally hundreds of German infantrymen were swarming over our dugouts and we were caught like rats in a trap. Within a few minutes we were all lined up on the road track by a German NCO and a platoon of men and there we joined all the French gunners in the vicinity who were already prisoners.

CCLI Brigade Headquarters was virtually taken prisoner to a man, including the CO, Lieutenant Colonel F B Moss-Blundell. The batteries of the brigade fared no better, the enemy had turned the flanks and they too were taken in the rear. The German guns had meticulously targeted each battery and all had suffered heavy casualties in their respective gun pits. A Battery fired at point blank at the advancing infantry at a range of sixty yards and all the guns were firing until the last minute. Most of the guns in the brigade were put out of action through hostile shelling and in the case of guns still workable after the German barrage had ceased, breech blocks and dial sights were removed. In many instances the enemy only managed to capture the battery positions after hand to hand fighting

The CCL Brigade was also subjected to the concentrated firepower of the German barrage. The commanding officer of the brigade, Lieutenant Colonel FDG Johnston, wrote to a colleague, Lieutenant Colonel HS Bell, on 28 May:

Gunner FW Long, A Battery, CCLI Brigade RFA. He survived the war.

At 1 am the Bosch opened a tremendous fire of high explosive and gas mixed so that we all had to stick in our gas proof dug outs and wear gas masks. Findlay, who was FOO [Forward Observation Officer]*, says the flashes of the guns were in a continuous line, and I think most of them must have been in the open, and so close up to the front line ... Findlay only saw for a minute or so, as the*

Bosch then put over smoke, and the wind was blowing straight towards the O P. There was also a heavy ground mist at dawn, so visibility was nil from the start. What happened to the infantry I have not yet heard, but I fancy they were pretty well scumfished [smothered] in the front line.

His barrage fire was wonderful and everybody caught it, even Divisional Headquarters, and of course he knew exactly where every battery and HQ and OP was. In the woods the gas soon became pretty bad and, wearing respirators, it was impossible to find your way in the dark. I was therefore unable to send any orderlies out till daybreak. The lines were absolutely gone by 1.15 am. I got one message through to Divisional Artillery and one to the batteries, before they went. Graham and linesmen tried to repair Infantry lines, but it was hopeless in the dark with respirators.

The howitzers of D Battery struggled to keep up a rate of twenty rounds per hour per gun through the German barrage. This battery was one of the few that had not been accurately targeted by the enemy and no howitzer was badly hit or ammunition set ablaze, but all lines of communication were cut and the guns continued to fire blind. However, the effects of the lingering gas began to take its toll, with many men collapsing in the gun pits; by 2.30 am there were only enough survivors to keep two howitzers in action. Finally, at 7 am, the remaining guns were overwhelmed by the German infantry and the guns were turned round and used by enemy gunners:

D Battery put up a fine fight, Darling and Earle, with two attached Infantry officers and a corporal, working the last gun, after all the rest of the battery were unconscious with gas, and Darling was last seen shooting at the Bosch with his revolver, while the other two worked the gun. It was of course impossible to get the guns away, as you could not possibly bring up horses.

A and B Batteries fought their guns until 6 am. Lieutenant Colonel Shiel of A Battery noticed the lifting barrage coming towards him and ordered breech blocks and sights to be removed and retired his men towards the Aisne. B Battery was quickly overwhelmed before appropriate measures could be carried out to render their guns ineffective, as was the case with C Battery, and almost all of the officers and men taken prisoner.

Profound confusion reigned over most of CCL Brigade's sector.

Bois de Beaumarais wood had been deluged in gas and the criss-crossing path and trackways to and from the individual battery operating positions added to the general chaos. All lines of communication had been cut. In this situation misunderstandings between units and divisional and brigade HQs were the inevitable result. Orders were sent out from divisional HQ to the gun lines at Glennes for horse limbers to be brought up to pull out the howitzers from D Battery. Their wagons were met by machine gun fire at close range, and only one member of the gun crew escaped. All the remaining men were killed, wounded or taken prisoner. A Battery's gun limbers almost shared a similar fate. Major Shiel recalled:

I ran, and ran, and ran, with the intention of making for DA and reporting. When I got out of the wood, and was making along the side of the hill towards Bearieux, where DA lived, a gentleman started sniping from the top of the hill, so I changed my tactics, and fled for the bridge. Within a mile of the river I picked up the rest of the Battery, retiring in good order, and suddenly, to my horror, discovered coming to meet us all the wagons and gun limbers. By screaming myself hoarse I got them halted, for they did not recognise their purple-faced, red eyed Battery Commander and, moreover, they had already been told that he was no more by the Sergeant-Major, who had incidentally pinched my horse! It did not take long to get the captain away at a gallop with the wagons for one bridge, nor for me to recapture my horse, get the limbers turned, and chase back to the other bridge. There was no time to be lost. As we came up to the bridge, two teams were shot down by our own shells; for the Germans had captured the Brigade on our left intact, and had turned their guns round and were firing on the bridge, and very accurately too.

Brigade Headquarters also had a narrow escape. The French officer who commanded the battery at Centre d'Evereux had alerted the Commanding Officer to the oncoming German Infantry. As Colonel Johnston noted:

About 7 30 am I found that the Bosch (sic) was in the wood on my right, and that the Infantry Brigadier had gone, so we had to burn our papers and clear, which we did only just in time, getting well machine-gunned when we reached the river, which we crossed about 10 am. The party consisted of Dickinson, Graham, Richardson, and myself, with six telephonists and four servants, and just as we got out of the wood Richardson, was hit badly and, I am sorry to say, he pegged out. We carried him several hundred yards through the Bosch barrage, which was very heavy, and there I found an old mattress-bed in a shanty, and we carried him on as far as Chaudardes, but when we got there he was dead. He was a most gallant fellow and did not know what fear was.

The losses of CCL Brigade were reported to be in the region of 160 killed, wounded and missing.

The CCLI Brigade's official record states:

At 1 am Division heavily attacked. All guns lost. Casualties of nineteen officers and 250 other ranks (chiefly missing). The whole of the brigade headquarters officers and records lost; at 10.30 am remains of Brigade moved via Fismes and St Gilles to Cohan.

Captain AH Leathart, CCL Brigade RFA and Major JG Leathart, 6/NF.

One of the officers of the CCLI Brigade marched into captivity was Lieutenant Witherington. He had initially been impressed by the swift advance of the Germans:

The activity behind what had been the German lines was amazing. Companies of infantry and batteries of guns were moving rapidly forward and there seemed to be miles of transport on the roads which had so recently been torn up by the barrage, but already made passable again by German Engineers.

However, on closer inspection the vehicles that had been pressed into service to serve the needs of the breakthrough were a very motley collection, and this in part explains why the German attack on the Aisne was not sustained with the same momentum on subsequent days. The contrast with British logistical support at this stage of the war was quite stark:

Enemy transport in use on this occasion was different from anything we had seen hitherto. Everything that could move on wheels had been put into commission and, mixed up with modern motor lorries, we saw every type of farm cart and even old cabs all heavily laden and drawn by horses, mules and oxen. It all doubtless served the purpose, which was to keep the advancing troops supplied with food and ammunition, but we saw nothing of the smartly turned out vehicles and well-fed, well-harnessed draught horses which were included in British lines of transport. It all seemed to point very clearly to the fact that the Germans were suffering from a great shortage of regular army transport.

Needless to say, all of the guns of both CCL and CCLI Brigades were lost, as it proved impossible to pull any out under the circumstances. By the end of the first day the 50th Division had been severely damaged, 227 officers and 4,879 other ranks were killed, wounded or captured on 27 May. A high proportion were PoWs, with as many as 153 infantry officers marched into captivity. There is no official figure for the number of other ranks who were made prisoner, but by using the number of officer PoWs as a guide the number could be as high as 4,000. The explanation given by the divisional historian, Everard Wyrall, was that: 'The majority were surrounded and forced to surrender before they could come into action.'

Of the three brigade commanders, Riddell (149) was severely wounded, Rees (150) was taken prisoner and Martin (151) was killed. At about midday on 27 May the remnants of the Division were organised into a composite unit under Colonels Walton and Kirkup, called the 149/151 Brigade Force. By the end of May the Division could only muster 700 fit infantry:

The 50th Division was broken, and although it was re-formed the new contained none of the old battalions. The 5,6 and 8 Durhams were reduced to a cadre on 15th June, all those surplus to cadre strength being distributed among other battalions.

The GOC, Major General Henry Jackson, wrote to his mother on 30 May outlining the plight of his division:

Just a line to say that I am alive and well. We have had rather a strenuous time – the Boche attack breaking in full force upon us. I have lost all my three Brigades and we are a poor affair at present, but given some men and a little time, we will be all right.

Despite the note of optimism on which the letter ends, this was to be the last action fought by the original 50th Division in the war. It was reconstituted and, as the historian of the 50th Division, Everard Wyrall, points out, its original identity was lost.

Chapter Three
THE DEFENCE OF THE WOODS AND
THE AISNE RIVER:
The 8th Division

The sector held by the 8th Division was different from that of the 50th Division in that the front line formed a right-angled salient, which projected out into the German positions. The topography of the sector was almost universally flat, but the terrain bore the scars from the fighting of previous years. Captain Sidney Rogerson, an officer attached to the headquarters of 23 Brigade, observed: 'The whole battle area had become a shrubbery, a vast garden fashioned by artillery.'

The right flank of the sector rested on the Aisne at the village of Berry-au-Bac. Another feature of this sector was the Miette stream, which was deep, about twenty feet wide and with very marshy banks. The Miette ran from front to rear, at right angles to the front. This served as the dividing line between the right and centre brigades, and was crossed by thirteen bridges. Instructions had been received on 7 May for the division to move into this sector and relieve the French *71st Division*, an operation that was duly carried out on 8 May. Divisional Headquarters were established at Roucy, three miles to the south of the Aisne.

The line taken over by the 8th Division on 12 May lay south of Juvincourt, the furthest point north east of the Allied line from Reims to Noyon. All three brigades were in the line, 25 right, 24 centre and 23 left. Each brigade had one battalion in the front line, one in support and one in reserve; each front line battalion had three companies in the forward trenches and one in reserve. The defensive positions occupied by the division consisted of an Outpost Line, in touch with the enemy, and a Battle Zone immediately in the rear. A line of redoubts, which in effect became the main line of

Lieutenant Colonel AE Eric Lowry, CO 2/West Yorks. At the time of his death at the age of 25 in September 1918, he was the youngest commanding officer on the Western Front.

resistance, screened the Battle Zone. The 8th Divisional History pointed out that:

> The orders from the French Command were that not a yard of ground was to be given up. The Outpost Line was to fight to the last. The Battle Zone was to be held at all costs, and all reserves were to be put in to retake any portion of this zone which might be lost to the enemy.

23 Brigade

On the morning of 27 May the Outpost Line was occupied by the 2/West Yorks. Three companies of the battalion held the front line with the remaining C Company in support under the direct control of Lieutenant Colonel Eric Lowry. The enemy bombardment, as predicted, commenced punctually at 1 am. During the hostile barrage the 2/West Yorks, in accordance with orders, evacuated the forward line and withdrew to the support trenches of the Outpost Line and there awaited the enemy's attack; in the hostile bombardment the battalion had already suffered heavy casualties. According to the war diary:

> It was 4.30 am when the enemy came over in very large numbers and though at a disadvantage owing to having to wear box respirators we promptly replied with machine-guns and rifle fire

Germany artillery in action.

and inflicted heavy losses on the enemy, who were temporarily held up.

It was not long before the battalion had lost touch with units to the left and right and the remaining troops fell back to the redoubt line. It was reported that barely twenty men got away; one of the few who managed to hobble back to safety was Colonel Lowry, with a gunshot wound in his foot.

The 2/Middlesex held the Battle Zone with two companies in the front line, one in a diagonal trench running back south-west and the fourth company in reserve in a redoubt covering the junction with the 50th Division to the left, situated just north of the village of La Ville-aux-Bois. The commanding officer, Lieutenant Colonel Charles Page, had ordered the trenches in this sector be improved in the days leading up to the attack, which helped to keep casualties to a minimum during the initial German bombardment:

I caused my battalion to construct sixteen half platoon trenches thirty feet in front of the front line with communication trenches back, nearly five feet deep with revetted fire steps. Only one trench had received a direct hit during the intense bombardment of five hours. Because of these trenches our casualties were comparatively light. We lost only three

Lieutenant Colonel CAS Page, CO, 2/Middlesex . In later life he served as a vicar in the south of England.

View from road to Juvincourt looking towards Musette Crossroads.

officers per company in line, and about four at Battalion Headquarters, sixteen officers in all. We suffered only one officer killed.

After an intense bombardment of the front line the barrage lifted on to the line of the Middlesex's headquarters in the gravel pit at La Ville-aux-Bois. All four companies reported at 6 am that the Germans had tried to advance and had been stopped due to a combination of rifle and machine gun fire. Soon after, men from the two front line companies were falling back on the defences held by C Company – the diagonal trench – which was attacked by enemy infantry coming from a north-westerly direction, through the defences held by the 149 Brigade. Colonel Page, overly anxious to ensure his front was ready to meet the German onslaught, took to patrolling each individual company. Captain Maberley Esler, Medical Officer of the 2/Middlesex, observed:

I was in a tunnel with the Colonel and Hugh. In the ordinary way Colonel Page should have remained there and runners would have reported from companies every few minutes and he would have directed orders as circumstances required. But no! He must go out himself and visit every sector of the defence. I remember him saying, 'I must go and see what all this bloody row is about!' Turning to Hugh he said, 'You deal with reports as they come in, and I will deal with events as I find them.' As he made his exit from the tunnel his last words were, 'Phew! What a bloody smell of gas! Look after yourself, Esler!' This is the last I ever saw of him.

Captain Servais del Court reported to Colonel Page a few minutes after 6 am that the Germans were only thirty yards from Battalion Headquarters just to the north of La Ville-aux-Bois. This required Colonel Page to take immediate action:

I sent out a half platoon of scouts to hold them up and ordered my headquarters and details to move to the redoubt held by Captain Worstall's [Wanstall] D Company. The shelling was so heavy and the Germans so close that it seemed doubtful if we should get through. I instructed each officer and man that the first to get through should ask Captain Worstall to make a counter-attack up C Company's trench with his right on the wire.

In attempting to pass on these instructions to Captain Leopold Wanstall, Colonel Page was badly wounded and later taken prisoner, but a Corporal Sensier managed to make his way to D Company. Colonel Page reported:

> *Corporal Sensier reached Captain Worstall and gave him my message. Sensier was shot through the head and killed as soon as he had given the message. Captain Worstall told me that Colonel Anderson-Morshead, 2nd Devons, was with him when he received my message. The Colonel had just come into Captain Worstall's redoubt. He formed up two companies of the 2nd Devons and Captain Worstall's 2nd Middlesex and advanced from the redoubt.*

Captain Leopold Wanstall, badly wounded and taken prisoner, lost an eye as a result of his injuries on the Aisne.

> *As soon as this counter-attack got out of the trench they were caught by machine gun fire. Colonel Morshead was killed and the three companies fell back into the trench. Captain Worstall rallied the men of both regiments and renewed the attempt to advance. He was almost at once shot through the eye, the men fell back to the trench and soon were all made prisoners. In the meantime, at about 6.30 am, I was made prisoner and was taken back to my own regimental aid post, which was in the hands of the Germans.*

Meanwhile Captain Esler had remained underground, waiting for reports of casualties. After the barrage ended he decided to investigate:

> *As I emerged into the open I smelt the early morning smell of mist and vegetation, with a pervading scent of cordite superimposed. I have never experienced the exact smell again, but I have remembered it all my life.*
>
> *As I came out, through the bushes emerged a few men with fixed bayonets, and an officer with a revolver in his hand. From their helmets I recognized that they were German, and that they were making a beeline for me. When the enemy break through they are excited and out to kill. If they see a man opposing them they shoot or charge with a bayonet. If they see a dugout they chuck a hand grenade in first before they investigate. As they came running the thought crossed my mind 'the possibility of being exterminated by a shell has been present with me often, but I never thought of ending my life with a bayonet wound in my*

belly, and I don't like the idea one little bit.' All I could do was shrug my shoulders and point at my Red Cross armlet. The officer recognized this at once and told his men not to kill. I pointed to my dugout and said 'Red Cross', and so they did not chuck in their usual grenades. Thus it was my instinct to don our Red Cross armlets that saved the lives of myself and my comrades in the aid post dugout.

Esler was beckoned to a British trench to give medical aid to victims of the recent attack:

A German map from 1916 of the Bois des Buttes, highlighting the complexity of tunnel trenches and craters

Skizze 13

I found the trench occupied by Germans, and in the bottom lay the dead and wounded and dying, some British and some German. There must have been a lot of hand-to-hand fighting, for many of them had bayonet wounds.

The German artillery and trench mortar barrage had had profound consequences upon the communication system within the command structure of the 8th Division. The 23 Brigade War Diary makes it clear that it was difficult to give precise timings for the events of the day, as most of the messages during the battle were lost. Rough estimates are given for the fall of the redoubt line at about 5 am and shortly afterwards the enemy were seen to be advancing on La Ville-aux-Bois. However, the diary indicates with a degree of certainty that 23 Brigade's positions within the Outpost and Battle Zone had fallen relatively early in the morning:

Between 5 am and 6 am it was clear that all our positions North of the Aisne were in the enemy's hands, and all of our batteries had, for at least two or three hours, been put out of action. What remained of the 23rd Brigade, together with Brigade Headquarters, withdrew across the Aisne by Pontavert under the close fire of the enemy's machine guns. About 6 am a position was taken up with what remained of the Brigade south of the Aisne above La Platterie.

The reserve battalion of 23 Brigade, 2/Devons, was stationed in the Bois des Buttes, a little to the south west of the village of La Ville-aux-Bois, on the morning of the attack. The stand made here by the 2nd Devons has become one of the most celebrated rearguard actions of the Great War. Even the commander's name, Lieutenant Colonel Rupert Henry Anderson-Morshead, has a Rorke's Drift ring about it. The Official History records that the 2/Devons, cited in French Army Orders, were awarded the Croix de Guerre, and they *had truly justified the regimental motto, 'Semper fidelis'. Many German battalions were required to dislodge it.* A Special Order No 4 of IX Corps noted:

On 27 May, after the enemy had captured our forward and main defences, the Second Devonshire Regiment maintained an unbroken front up to a late hour in the morning. Although surrounded and repeatedly attacked, it successfully defeated all attempts of the enemy to advance on its front… There is no doubt that this Battalion perished en masse. It refused to surrender and fought to the last.

British dead in the Bois des Buttes.

The day before the attack, 26 May, the 2/Devons were in Brigade Reserve at Roucy. At 8 pm the battalion was ordered to move north through Pontavert to the Bois des Buttes, where they were to form the garrison of the battle line. The Bois des Buttes was a small hill with two little pimples for summits. Underneath lay a labyrinth of tunnels and large dugouts. Captain Rogerson of 23 Brigade Headquarters, which was also in the Bois des Buttes, describes the extent of this elaborate underground defensive network:

> *Except for its topographical prominence, the Bois des Buttes was an ideal headquarters. Around its base deep shafts led down to a regular underground barracks, thirty feet below ground level, excavated originally by the enemy and improved by the French. Apart from the burrows actually running under the hillock itself and occupied by the personnel of Brigade Headquarters, were three other sets of tunnels, all lighted by electricity and big enough if necessary to hide three battalions, in addition to the heterogeneous collection of British artillery observers and French electrical mechanics, anti-tank gunners, and heavy machine gunners located in them. Indeed, an entire German regiment had, we are told, been, found in them when taken a year previously. They had since been much enlarged and improved,*

and there were two entrances into which ran miniature railways and big enough to allow the passage of a three ton lorry. The Bois des Buttes was in short a defensive position of great potential strength. The trouble was that its vast and ramified systems of tunnels was never half-explored nor a quarter used.

The reconnoitring of the dug out positions for the Devons was given to Captain Rogerson and Captain Philip Ledward – also from the staff of 23 Brigade. Rogerson observed: 'The Devons had never seen the position or been in the tunnels, and as they would arrive after dark we dared not imagine how they were likely to fare.'

However, the deep dugouts and tunnels of the Bois des Buttes occupied by the 2/Devons during the opening phase of the bombardment afforded them much better protection than the forward positions occupied by fellow battalions of 23 Brigade. Although uncomfortable in their gas

Private Reg Gingell, 2/Middlesex, taken prisoner on 27 May.

masks, the Devons remained safe from the vast amount of HE and gas shells that were exploding overhead.

23 Brigade Headquarters remained in contact with both 149 Brigade of the 50th Division to the left and 24 Brigade to the right during the course of the bombardment, but no news was received that the enemy had attacked, even as dawn was breaking. Within the space of ten to fifteen minutes this situation altered dramatically. Captain Thompson – 23 Brigade Staff Captain – from his observation post on the Bois des Buttes, stated that he had seen German observation balloons rising from the British front line. Two messages followed: 24 Brigade reported that the enemy was advancing up the Miette stream, close to their Brigade Headquarters, and a communiqué from 149 Brigade provided information that the *'Enemy has broken our battle line and is advancing on La Ville-aux-Bois.'* Rogerson states that both these messages were received at about 5.30 am. This created a degree of panic and confusion in brigade headquarters:

Our position was no longer a stronghold but a death trap. There was nothing left but to obey orders and fall back across the Aisne - a decision no sooner made than acted upon. Men struggled into their battle equipment as they clambered up the steep stairs… What a scene met us as we floundered into the light of the young

107

day! Everything was ruin, desolation thinly veiled by mist and smoke. The barrage had begun to lift a little but was still very heavy, and the line of the Aisne spouted black where big shells were bursting.

In this desperate scramble to vacate Brigade Headquarters, it would appear that no orders were given to the 2/Devons to assume battle stations. As dawn broke at 3.45 am Colonel Anderson-Morshead decided to leave the underground shelters and occupy the trenches above. Earlier, emerging from their dugouts at about 4 am, the Devons had been met by a heavy attack from German infantry supported by aeroplanes. Three companies took up positions on the northern edge of the Bois des Buttes whilst one company was kept in reserve. The Devons were quickly engaged with the enemy, who were advancing in large numbers. D Company of the 2/Middlesex acting in a like manner was overcome. The Devons fought on until superior numbers of German troops, who had managed to advance through a gap which had opened up due to the destruction of 149 Brigade to the left, were able to turn the flank and envelop the 2/Devons from the rear. As a result three companies of the Devons were destroyed. Colonel Anderson-Morshead managed to rally the support company and hold the Bois des Buttes for a period of time, before it was decided that a fighting withdrawal to the Aisne was the only option due to the overwhelming numbers of enemy troops now attacking them.

More detailed and dramatic accounts of the action fought by the 2/Devons on the Bois des Buttes are provided by both the *History of the Devonshire Regiment*, by C T Atkinson, *The 8th Division in War 1914–1918* by Boraston and Bax (published in 1926) and a memoir of the 2/Devons in 1918 by Reginald Colwill, *Through Hell to Victory: From Passchendaele to Mons with the 2/Devons in 1918* (1927). Colwill fought with the Devons during this period. All of these works highlight the heroic nature of the struggle played by all companies of the Devons which allowed Brigadier General George William St. George Grogan, GOC the 23 Brigade, time to organise a defence on the high ground south of the Aisne. Atkinson's version of events describes the confused nature of the fighting:

Exact details of what happened are hard to obtain. The survivors have carried away but confused and incoherent recollections of the hell in which the battalion fought and perished, and it is very difficult to piece together the story from fragmentary and imperfect evidence.

Second Lieutenant W Candler, 2/Devons, one of nineteen Devon officers taken prisoner, 27 May.

This is reflected in the inconsistencies in the documentation of the events of the battle, the engagement of other battalions, the timescales and the casualties suffered.

It seems likely that the fighting in the Bois des Buttes degenerated into a number of small-scale actions waged by platoons or even individual soldiers themselves. The nature of the terrain – the warren of underground tunnels – and the destruction wrought by the German bombardment had all contributed to isolated groups of soldiers desperately holding out against superior enemy forces, or being forced to surrender. This appears to have been the case with the three companies of the 2/Devons who had been ordered to take up their positions on the northern edge of the Bois des Buttes. In a letter to General Sir George Bullock (Colonel of the Devonshire Regiment), Brigadier General Grogan quotes an unnamed eyewitness who saw the regiment, 'though merely an island in the midst of an innumerable foe … fighting with perfect discipline, and by the steadiness of their fire, mowing down the enemy in large numbers'.

The last action of the 2/Devons on the morning of 27 May was the stand made by Colonel Anderson-Morshead and the remnants of the reserve company. According to Atkinson, at 9.30 am the Colonel and Adjutant, with less than fifty men of the support company, led a charge down the hill to attack German artillery who were coming up the road from Juvincourt. It was at this point that Major B W Ellis, the CO of the 57th Battery XLV Brigade RFA joined the Devons. His testimony, given to 8th Division Headquarters, provided the evidence that led to the IX Corps Special Order No 4 and the granting of the Croix de Guerre:

At a late hour in the morning I, with those of my men who had escaped the enemy machine guns and his fearful barrage, joined the CO of the 2nd Devonshire Regiment, and a handful of men holding onto the last trench north of the canal. They were in a position in which they were entirely without hope of help but were fighting on grimly. The Commanding Officer himself was calmly writing his notes with a perfect hail of high explosive falling round him. I spoke to him and he told me that nothing could be done. He refused all offers of help from my artillerymen, who were unharmed, and sent them off to get through if they could. His magnificent courage, dauntless bearing and determination to carry on to the end moved one's emotions.

Some time after this Anderson-Morshead was killed. In ushering one group of men to join the others across the Juvincourt road he was shot by a machine gun bullet. Very few men remained and most were now taken prisoner. According to WJP Aggett, in his relatively recent history of the Devonshire Regiment:

So ended the fight at the Bois des Buttes which began at about 4 am and lasted until sometime after 12.30 pm on 27 May 1918, during which twenty-three officers and 528 men were killed or posted as missing.

Somewhere between fifty and eighty men managed to escape across the Aisne to form the nucleus of a company that was preparing to take up defensive positions on the high ground under the command of Second Lieutenant Clarke.

On 5 December 1918 the Croix de Guerre was presented to the 2/Devons at a ceremonial parade by General de Laguishe. The citation reads:

On 27 May 1918, North of the Aisne, at a time when the British Trenches were being subjected to fierce attacks, the 2nd Battalion Devonshire Regiment repelled successive enemy assaults with gallantry and determination, and maintained an unbroken front till a late hour. Inspired by the sangfroid of their gallant Commander, Lieutenant Colonel R H Anderson Morshead, DSO, in the face of an intense bombardment, the few survivors of the Battalion, though isolated and without hope of assistance, held on to their trenches North of the River and fought to the last with an unhesitating obedience to Orders. The staunchness of this Battalion permitted the defences South of the Aisne to be organised and their occupation by reinforcements to be completed. Thus the whole Battalion – Colonel, twenty-eight Officers, and 552 Non-Commissioned Officers and men – responded with one accord and offered their lives in ungrudging sacrifice to the sacred cause of the Allies.

(signed) Berthelot – General Commanding Fifth Army

A representation of Lieutenant Colonel R H Anderson-Morshead's last stand. He is shown here calmly writing orders in the midst of carnage unfolding all around.

The 2/Devons were the only infantry unit to receive such an honour for their actions on 27 May.

Other sources, whilst acknowledging the bravery of the Devons, highlight that they were not the only battalions engaged in this action. In 1934 Lieutenant Colonel Page, of the 2/Middlesex, wrote to Sir James Edmonds with his reflections on a draft of the Official History he had been sent. He was concerned that the role of his battalion had not been adequately represented:

> *My Dear General,*
>
> *I enclose a detailed account of what happened on 27 May and a brief suggested draft for the history. The account I give is my own up to my sending the order for counter-attack by Worstall* [Acting Captain Leopold Wanstall] *Do please either use my evidence (? Unsupported!!- as suggested!!), or make a close enquiry from*

others, Captain Worstall 2nd Middlesex Regiment or officer survivors of the 8th Divisional Machine Gun Battalion.

For we felt very sore in the 2nd Middlesex Regiment about this battle. We saw all the accounts of the Devons. They did well no doubt - but as prisoners we knew that most of their officers were taken unwounded, and two or one and a half companies were taken still in the tunnels in the Bois des Buttes and were never engaged.

Another officer, Captain Ledward of 23 Brigade who, along with Captain Rogerson, had been responsible for guiding the 2/Devons in the tunnels of the Bois des Buttes, also reports that a large number of the Devons were trapped under the Buttes and made captive. Nevertheless, he had nothing but praise for the role of Anderson-Morshead:

He deserved his fame. He could have got back over the Aisne, as we of the 23rd HQ staff got back, but he refused to do so. He collected what men he could find and refused to surrender and was duly killed.

The 'suggested draft for the official history' submitted by Colonel Page provides further detail of the part played by Captain Wanstall and the reserve Company of the 2/Middlesex:

The 2nd Middlesex held the Battle Zone with two companies in the front line, one in a diagonal trench running back south west and the fourth (reserve) company in a redoubt covering the point

Men of the 2/Devons at home. Private WH Daniel, second row, second from right, was killed on 30 May.

of junction with the 50th Division. The diagonal trench was broken through by 6 am and the battalion HQ occupied. Lieutenant Colonel Page was severely wounded and taken prisoner. The reserve company was ordered by Colonel Page to make a counter-attack up the diagonal trench. Lieutenant Colonel Anderson-Morshead, 2nd Devons, was with Captain Worstall (reserve company 2nd Middlesex Regiment) when he received this order. He led two of his companies and Captain Worstall's company in this counter-attack and was killed. Captain Worstall rallied the Devons and Middlesex and renewed the counter-attack. He was severely wounded in the head and the counter-attack was abandoned. The two front companies, 2nd Middlesex, held the line against great odds by rifle and Lewis gun fire and prevented any German advance till about 10 am. They were captured by Germans coming from the rear who had broken through the 50th Division front. Not one unwounded man of the companies crossed the Aisne.

The account by Colonel Page is at odds with the version of events provided in the 8th Divisional History, the Devonshire Regimental History and also the Official History. Edmonds does mention, albeit briefly, the role of the reserve company, D, of the Middlesex. But there is no reference to Captain Wanstall rallying the Devons and Middlesex following the death of Anderson-Morshead, possibly because he failed to find Wanstall and have the story verified.

Interestingly, the capture statement made by Captain HL MacIlwaine, Adjutant of the 2/Middlesex, on 26 January 1919 reports:

I reached Brigade HQ about 7 am and found the place deserted. Found many papers etc lying about, which I burnt, as the Germans were advancing rapidly. About 8 am I came under orders of the CO of the Devons of our Brigade. He had about fifty men, which he divided up between another officer, himself and myself. We endeavoured to fight our way back to the Aisne, but owing to the Germans having gained the high ground we got little chance of giving shot for shot, and it was almost fatal to show a finger. The Devons' CO was killed almost instantly. By belly crawling in short grass for 300 yards and bolting from shell hole to shell hole a few of us managed to make our way to the outskirts of Pontavert, most of my men having been wiped out by the most deadly machine gun and rifle fire. At 2 pm I found myself just on the wrong side of the Aisne and its canal...surrounded on all sides

A German photograph of destroyed British trenches in the 'Viller wald', the Bois des Buttes. (Liddle Collection)

by overwhelming numbers…I decided there was no alternative but to surrender.

Nonetheless, in all of the histories mentioned above regarding the charge led by Anderson-Morshead and his subsequent death, there is no mention – even by eyewitnesses in the primary sources used by Aggett and Colwill – of any role played by the Middlesex: it was purely a Devons affair.

There are also discrepancies in the various accounts over the length of time the Devons managed to hold off the Germans on the Bois des Buttes. Major BW Ellis, the battery commander who witnessed Anderson-Morshead rallying the reserve company of the 2/Devons believes that the action took place at a *late hour in the morning*. Aggett confirms this in his history of the Devonshire Regiment and also maintains that remnants of the Devons, after the death of Anderson-Morshead, continued to fight until *some time after 12.30 pm*. The time thus gained proved to be crucial, as it slowed down the German advance in this sector and allowed an organised defence to be arranged by British reserves south of the Aisne. Again this version of events differs in many respects from Colonel Page's assessment of the battle on the morning of the attack. In his view, not only was it the 2/Middlesex who offered the last vestiges of resistance in 23 Brigade's sector, but the counter attacks led by Anderson-Morshead and Wanstall took place between 6 am and 7 am. Undoubtedly there had been stubborn resistance in the vicinity of the Bois des Buttes and the Butte de l'Edmond on the morning of 27 May, but to a large extent this was of little consequence. The forward companies of the 158th German Infantry Regiment had reached Pontavert and the Aisne by 8 am and a German artillery officer remembers his battery reaching the village by noon.

Inevitably given the speed of this advance, many prisoners were taken. A number of German accounts speak of the large number of English prisoners taken in the area of the Bois des Buttes; it is likely that a fair proportion of these were from the 2/Devons. In fact no official figures exist for the number of other ranks taken prisoner from the Devonshire Regiment on 27 May, but the numbers would have been substantial if the numbers of officers taken captive are any guide. 2/Devons had twenty officers made PoW on 27 May. Furthermore, four were killed – including Colonel Anderson-Morshead – out of twenty-eight officers at the beginning of the battle. The number of other ranks killed in action was also comparatively small. The CWGC records shown that twenty-five of the 2/Devons were killed in action on the day of the attack; this figure rises to eighty-three deaths if we take into consideration the days that followed, up until 1 June.

But this is not to denigrate Anderson-Morshead and the reserve company of the 2/Devons and remnants of the 2/Middlesex who fought bravely until overpowered by irresistible numbers.

The stand made by the 2/Devons has been immortalised through a simple stone cross in front of the Mairie of La Ville-aux-Bois. Engraved on the plinth is the citation for the Croix de Guerre. 27 May had been a disaster for the IX Corps and in particular for the 8th and 50th Divisions. As pointed out by Sidney Rogerson in *The Last of the Ebb:*

History will never know the details of the deadly isolated struggles which must have been fought out in the mists and marshes of the Aisne. Time and the evidence of chance witnesses have lifted the curtain sufficiently to allow us a glimpse here and there. One such glimpse reveals the stand of the 2nd Devons in front of Pontavert.

The chance eyewitness in the case of the Devons was Major Ellis, whose report reached 8th Division and, subsequently, IX Corps

"Die Elisabether in Bereitschaft-Stellung bei Corbeny."

3rd Garde Grenadiers (Queen Elisabeth Regiment) near Corbeny before the attack launched against the 8th Division.

Headquarters. Because of the calamitous nature of the fighting, few reports from front line units reached Divisional, let alone Corps Headquarters. There had been praiseworthy stands made by other units, such as the 4/NF under Colonel Gibson at the Butte de l'Edmond; but many brave actions were only witnessed by men from the same company or battalion and as a result were not given the credit they deserved in the form of an official reward.

Nevertheless, in recognition of the heroic sacrifice of so many men on such a disastrous day for the British Army, something had to be salvaged. As a result certain units were singled out and have subsequently attained heroic status: the 2/Devons at the Bois des Buttes and the stand made by 5th Battery, XLV Brigade, Royal Field Artillery. There was also a need in the dark days of the German offensives of March, April and May to raise morale, and units like the Devons at the Bois des Buttes, 16/Manchesters at Manchester Hill and 4/Grenadier Guards at Hazebrouk, served as models of courage holding out against the German onslaught; in the words of Brigadier General Grogan:

> *The undaunted courage of these gallant men, their unbroken front and high morale, was throughout an example and an inspiration*

116

to the less stout-hearted and the despondent, and I consider their conduct worthy of the highest praise.

The recognition of the sacrifice by the IX Corps on the banks of the Aisne was also acknowledged by the French authorities, when both the 2/Devons and the 5th Battery were awarded the Croix de Guerre. Perhaps this had to be the case; as Rogerson points out: 'This was the first act of the unified command on the Western Front.'

Conceivably it was also a tacit acknowledgement that French orders had placed British units in such a woeful defensive position that once attacked a catastrophe was the inevitable outcome. Heroism alone could not save the day.

24 Brigade

24 Brigade held the centre of the 8th Division's position, with three companies of 2/Northamptons in the front line and another company a few hundred yards to the rear, holding the outer reaches of the Battle Zone. The officer commanding the Northamptonshires, the uncompromising Lieutenant Colonel Christopher G Buckle, sent his last message to the forward companies just after the German bombardment commenced:

> *All Platoon Commanders will remain with their platoons and ensure that the trenches are manned immediately the bombardment lifts. Send short situation wire every half-hour. No short bombardment can possibly cut our wire and if the sentries are alert it cannot be cut by hand. If they try it, shoot the devils.*
>
> *C G Buckle, Lieut.-Col*

2/Northamptons were gradually driven back to the Battle Zone where they joined with 1/Worcesters. According to the 8th Divisional History, the position here was so strong that any frontal assault would have been repelled, but the enemy managed to turn the right flank. The trenches were well sited, with views across the level ground from the main road at Berry-au-Bac to Corbeny. The mist that had accumulated in the Miette valley assisted the attacking troops, along with the five captured Mark IV tanks from Assault Tank Detachment 12 (which supported 158th Infantry Regiment) that began to penetrate the defensive positions of the Worcesters by 5 am. Captain HF Stacke's *History of the Worcestershire Regiment* provides the following narrative of the collapse of the Battle Zone:

The anti-tank guns smashed the German tanks at point blank range, while the enemy's infantry, disordered after their battle in the forward trenches, were beaten off again and again by rapid fire of musketry and machine guns. Confident reports were sent back that the Battalion was holding its ground, and all seemed well when, through the mist, more tanks and fresh waves of the enemy's infantry came surging up from the right rear against the flank of the 1st Worcestershire. The battalions of the 25th Brigade had been overrun, and the victorious enemy was rolling up the defensive line. In a short time the Battalion was surrounded and attacked in front, flank and rear. Major Cartland, [father of novelist Barbara Cartland] *commanding the Battalion, was killed in the trenches with his men.*

The anti-tank guns used here were French 75s of the 176th Regiment. Four tanks were knocked out, with the fifth suffering engine trouble that led it to stall.

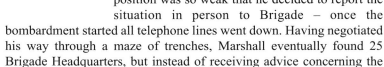

Major JB Cartland.

Towards the rear of the Battle Zone there seems to have been considerable confusion. Captain RC Marshall, commanding D Company of the 1/Worcesters, had been instructed on the evening of 26 May that his unit was to be relieved by a company of 1/Sherwood Foresters, who were in brigade reserve near Roucy. Pending the arrival of the relief unit, Marshall held his front with a skeleton company and sent the remainder of his troops to Battalion Headquarters, as commanded. However, 1/Sherwood Foresters never arrived, and the front here was held very thinly when the German attack began. Captain Marshall was so concerned that the defensive position was so weak that he decided to report the situation in person to Brigade – once the bombardment started all telephone lines went down. Having negotiated his way through a maze of trenches, Marshall eventually found 25 Brigade Headquarters, but instead of receiving advice concerning the displacement of his troops, he became responsible for the organisation of a makeshift defence:

There was a deep trench near here and my recollection is of a confused mass of men of many different regiments. Events then happened rapidly. Another officer and myself tried to organise

A posed photograph of British soldiers from the 24 Brigade with their captors, 27 May, near Juvincourt.

the men and get them extended along the line of the parapet of the trench, as there were shouts that the Germans were coming over. I remember getting hold of a Lewis gun myself and getting on the parapet of the trench.

One of the other units involved in this confused mass of men was a company of the 22nd Durham Light Infantry, a Pioneer battalion. This unit had been in support of the 1/Worcesters but had been ordered forward to stem the German advance. At 5 am the reserve battalion, the 1/Sherwood Foresters, was also ordered to move from near Roucy to occupy a position to the south of 25 Brigade Headquarters, but they never crossed the Aisne. Advanced units of the German infantry who had begun to occupy the north bank of the river fired upon them. Instead the Sherwood Foresters began to deploy along the canal adjacent to the Bois de Gernicourt. It was now 7 am and by the time they had reached the northern edge of the wood all of the bridges in this sector, except one, had been blown by the engineers.

Meanwhile the remnants of 24 Brigade had fallen back to La Pêcherie Bridge and a defence was organised by Captain Acton Brooke Pratt, adjutant of 1/Worcesters. However, the enemy worked their way behind Captain Pratt's party and cut them off. A few managed to escape

British PoWs carry a wounded comrade near Berry-au-Bac.

over the river and canal; by 9 am only three officers and sixty-eight other ranks remained of the brigade, holding a trench north of Roucy.

25 Brigade

The sector occupied by 25 Brigade on the morning of 27 May was the most vulnerable to enemy attack. The brigade area formed a salient on the right flank of the Chemin des Dames position and faced north-east to south-east. Furthermore, this sector was enclosed on the left by the Miette and on the right by the Aisne. It was a low lying, marshy area, where mist accumulated in the depressions and hollows. The 2/Royal Berkshires, to the left, and 2/Rifle Brigade, to the right, each had two companies in the front line. Two further companies of the Rifle Brigade were stationed adjacent to the Aisne, overlooking the flood plain and canal, facing in a south easterly direction.

To the south, guarding Berry-au-Bac and the road from Pontavert to Guignicourt, was the Battle Zone. This area was to be held in half company or platoon posts, which were adapted for all round defence. This was a necessary defensive precaution given the exposed nature of 25 Brigade's position. Most of the posts were in good repair, but the

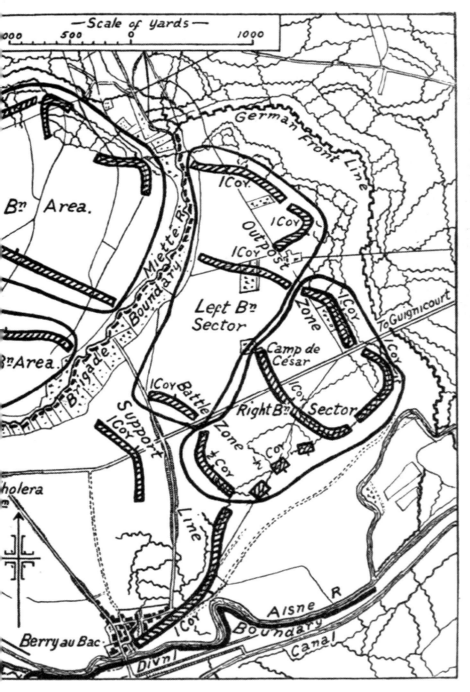

25 Brigade sector: 2/Royal Berks and 2/Rifle Brigade in the front line with 2/East Lancs in reserve

area was a labyrinth of disused trenches, some of which had been filled with wire to prevent enemy penetration. On 26 May this region was held extremely lightly by two companies of 1/Worcesters. At 5.30 pm on the day preceding the attack, Lieutenant Colonel Gerald Hill, CO of 2/East Lancs, received a telephone message from Divisional Headquarters that an attack was expected. Two companies of 2/East Lancs were directed to move at once from brigade reserve at Guyencourt to relieve 1/Worcesters in the Battle Zone. Guyencourt was five miles in the rear and by the time A and C Companies were met by guides at Gernicourt it was after midnight. This proved a costly error: C Company was directed to make the change over with 1/Worcesters near 25 Brigade Headquarters just as the German bombardment commenced at 1 am. Committed to fighting almost immediately on arrival in the Battle Zone, the company sustained very heavy casualties. The fate of A Company was much the same. The guides that met the company lost their way through the bewildering network of trenches. When the company eventually reached their defensive positions – two hours behind schedule – they had already incurred heavy casualties due to the enemy's preliminary bombardment. Moreover, they found the front line here – covering Berry-au-Bac – deserted, and before they had time to organise an effective resistance the position was attacked by overwhelming numbers of enemy troops and the company of 2/East Lancs was practically annihilated.

Colonel GEM Hill, O 2/East Lancs. A caric drawn whilst in capt

The German infantry deployed opposite 25 Brigade took advantage of the flat terrain and the low lying mist. The assault battalions of the enemy, accompanied by commandeered British tanks, delivered their opening attack at 4 am at the apex of the salient against both troops from the Berkshires and the Rifle Brigade. The tanks were used to flatten out the wire, allowing the German shock troops to pinch out both sides of the exposed British outpost positions. The two front line battalions were overrun within an hour; the misty conditions aiding the aggressor. Such was the chaos generated that little communication was possible with headquarters in the rear, except by pigeon post:

It is only at intervals that a clear message comes back out of the confusion which the fog necessarily produced. Even such a message only serves to emphasise the assistance which the lack of visibility and the exposed position of our troops in the salient gave to the enemy in attack. Take, for instance, the following message, timed at 5.15 am, which was received at Divisional Headquarters at 6 am: 'HQ 2nd Berks...surrounded. Germans threw bombs down dugouts and passed on. Appeared to approach from right rear in considerable strength. No idea what has happened elsewhere. Holding out in hope of relief.'

As the German forward units quickly swept past the outpost zone, the Battle Zone was attacked early in this sector. Brigade Headquarters were surrounded before news had reached Brigadier General Ralph Husey that the front line had collapsed. At 5 am a telephone message from Division was sent to the two remaining companies of 2/East Lancs, now in Gernicourt Wood, to move northwards to the Battle Zone, near to Brigade Headquarters. By now complete confusion reigned in the forward areas and the Battle Zone. Lieutenant Colonel Hill, accompanied by his adjutant and two orderlies, moved on ahead of B and D Companies of 2/East Lancs to reconnoitre the situation north of the river and make contact with Brigade Headquarters. This turned out to be a disaster. Both Hill and his second in command were taken prisoner:

Captain W Lowe, 2/East Lancs, KiA, 27 May.

After crossing the Aisne we took the 'up' trench and got to within 300 yards of Brigade Headquarters where the trench was blown in and we had to get out of the trench. To my utter astonishment I found myself in the middle of a party of Germans; an officer and a dozen men were within two or three paces of me and another party of about a hundred men under a captain was fifty yards away...I had no time to draw my revolver nor had my adjutant who was close to me. This happened at 6.50 am and at this time no guns on our side were firing.

The capture of Lieutenant Colonel Hill illustrates very effectively the almost total breakdown of communication within 25 Brigade and between 25 Brigade and Divisional Headquarters. He had received no information about events north of the Aisne - except for the order from division that the troops from his two companies were needed to defend the Battle Zone. Wounded officers and men, whom he met on the way up, gave no intimation that the enemy had broken through, but rather conveyed the impression that all was going well. It would appear that no messengers were sent down the 'up' trench to report to Hill about events near the front; some French artillery men, who were met just south of the Aisne, seemed quite happy but complained they had nothing to aim at. Finally, the Brigade Intelligence Officer, carrying an order to Colonel Hill to remain on the south bank of the Aisne, missed him but delivered the message to the two companies concerned and thereby averted complete disaster.

Private L A Page, fought with the 8/MGC and survived the war.

Serious mistakes had been made in the 8th Divisional area. The most profound of these were the undefended front line north of Berry-au-Bac that had been encountered by the two forward companies of the 2/East Lancs when they moved to take position during the early hours of 27 May. This sector had been held by the 1/Worcesters, from 24 Brigade, but it would appear they had been ordered to move back to positions within their own brigade area prior to the enemy attack. This left an undefended gap in one of the most exposed areas of the entire British front line. The advancing German infantry took full advantage of this. A and C Companies of the 2/East Lancs who were moving up - in effect to plug the gap - were swept aside. The remaining battalions of 25 Brigade in the forward trenches were cut off and the momentum of the enemy advance carried them into the Battle Zone of 24 Brigade, effectively rolling up the defensive line from the right flank. 25 Brigade Headquarters narrowly escaped being taken prisoner en masse. The Brigade Major, Basil Pascoe, was killed organising a retreat to the south. Brigadier General

A section of the 8/MGC, Private Page is sitting front row, second from the right.

Husey and what was left of his staff reached Gernicourt Wood and set to work managing a line of resistance to the south of the Aisne with the few survivors of his brigade who had struggled to fight their way to the river.

A good deal of the responsibility for these defensive shortcomings must be attached to the commander of the 8th Division, Major General William Heneker. He had allotted Brigadier General Husey a sector of the front line that was by far the most vulnerable to attack of all the brigade areas under the control of the Division. Husey was undoubtedly a brave soldier and leader but was a relatively inexperienced brigade commander. However, he was expected to hold an important sector with at least two seriously degraded units - 2/Rifle Brigade and the 2/Berkshires – both units were relative newcomers, having only joined the brigade in early May.

Lack of effective communication across brigade boundaries was another weakness that was highlighted during the morning of the attack. No messages appear to have been passed between the 24 and 25 Brigade Headquarters – or they were lost – during what should have been a relatively easy change over between 1/Worcesters and the 2/East Lancs on the evening of 26 May. The responsibility for this must rest on both the staff of both brigades and the staff of the division itself and ultimately, of course, on the divisional commander. As the First World War historian, John Bourne pointed out:

British prisoners being led through a communication trench towards Juvincourt.

The [8th] division disintegrated during a leaderless rout. Heneker performed no great acts of generalship. The successive events in which he found himself were exceptionally demanding, physically, mentally and morally. It was very difficult to find out what was happening, even after personal reconnaissance.

The 8th Divisional Royal Field Artillery

The Official History is laconic in the extreme with regards to the performance of the 8th Division's two Royal Field Artillery brigades on 27 May: 'The 8th Division artillery (Brigadier General J Lamont) met with the same fate as that of the 50th Division. All the field guns in action, both British and French, were lost.'

A footnote provides a few rudimentary details of the performance of the individual batteries of XXXIII and XLV Brigades. Many guns were destroyed in the opening phase of the German preliminary

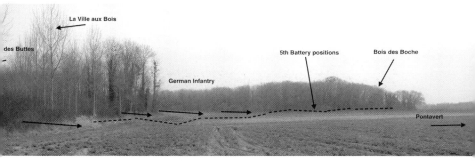

La Ville aux Bois

des Buttes

5th Battery positions

Bois des Boche

German Infantry

Pontavert

The attack against the 5 Battery 45 Brigade RFA.

bombardment. At 2.15 am the German guns, which had been occupied with attacking Allied positions across the Aisne, concentrated their fire on British and French artillery emplacements. By 8 am at the latest all seventy-six guns of the 8th Division had been overrun.

The positions occupied by the British artillery batteries were well known to the Germans. For instance, on 12 May the 5th Field Battery – part of XLV Brigade – took over positions to the south of Bois des Buttes vacated by a unit of French 75 mm guns, who had been in line for a number of months. The remaining batteries of XLV Brigade were clustered around the area of the Bois des Boche and to the south of La Ville-aux-Bois, covering the zone of 23 Brigade. 24 Brigade was covered by the guns of XXXIII Brigade, which were stationed near the Aisne at La Pêcherie. Finally, on the right, the zone containing 25 Brigade was supported by a group of French 75 mm guns, located to the south of the Aisne.

Lieutenant Colonel John Ballard was particularly critical of the location of the gun pits occupied by the batteries of XLV Brigade. As commanding officer of this unit, he had requested permission from the Divisional Commander of the Royal Artillery (CRA), Brigadier General JWF Lamont, to change the positions of his batteries some ten days prior to the attack, but this had been denied:

I incurred the displeasure of my superiors by suggesting some weeks previously that I left one gun in the wretched old French gun pits we had been ordered to occupy, for I wanted to place the remainder hidden and never fired until there was a severe affair. This was frowned upon. In fact, on a quiet sector, I was ordered to fire hundreds of rounds during the week in order to support the morale of the infantry. This sector was perfectly peaceful and apparently deserted.

Steps were taken to offset the vulnerability of the location of the artillery batteries to German counter battery fire by building more reliable and solid field defences during the fortnight leading up to the German attack. For example, 5th Battery's guns were deployed in two sections of three, each with a sandbag parapet built to the front and sides for greater protection against impact. The Battery Commander, Major JC Griffiths, had also overseen the construction of a better than adequate system of local defence trenches. However, not all the batteries had been as diligent as the 5th Battery in its preparation of defences.

The precision of the German bombardment on the morning of 27 May as regards counter battery location and destruction was devastating. According to the history of the 8th Division, the enemy knew all the battery and gun pit positions and were therefore heavily shelled, at first with gas shells and later with a mixture of HE and gas, *and the enemy shooting seemed uncannily accurate.* Within XLV Brigade RFA, approximately twenty guns were destroyed in the opening salvoes of the German attack. Under these conditions, the counter-preparation and harassing fire of the British artillery, which should have continued all night, proved in many cases impossible to carry out. The rapid advance of German infantry units was equally catastrophic. Between 6 and 7 am men of both XLV and XXXIII brigades were involved in desperate hand-to-hand fighting in the gun pits. In the 1st Battery (XLV) four guns were put out of action by the

German tank 'Paul', of Abteilung 12, knocked out by artillery fire near La Ville-Aux-Bois. (Rainier Strasheim)

preliminary bombardment. By 7 am this position was enveloped and subsequently overrun, but not before breech blocks had been removed and the defenders had engaged the enemy in vicious close combat using Lewis guns and rifles. Only two NCOs and six men got away. The history records the demise of 32 Battery (XXXIII Brigade):

Major AG Ramsden, the Battery Commander, had one of his guns run out of its emplacements, so as to give it a wider arc of fire, and with it kept the enemy off at close range, the remaining gunners and NCOs assisting with Lewis gun and rifle fire. The gun was eventually placed on a small railway truck; and, after all maps, records, kits, etc, which could not be removed had been burnt and other guns had been rendered useless by the removal of breech blocks and sights, Major Ramsden retired down the Miette Valley, fighting a rearguard action with his one gun. Although nearly surrounded and ultimately forced to abandon his gun, he was finally able to get the remaining personnel of his battery across the canal.

Major JC Griffiths, CO of 5 Battery, had taken the opportunity in the relative calm of the Chemin des Dames sector to enjoy a few days' rest in the rear area. One of the battery's guns had also been sent to a workshop for repair. On the eve of battle the battery was now under the temporary command of Captain John H Massey. He ensured that everything had been done to allow the guns to fire throughout the night. Ammunition for immediate use was stored next to each gun in a two wheeled caisson positioned under the parapet. More ammunition was kept to the rear of the gun platform in a pit specifically dug for that purpose. The guns assumed battle positions in two sections of three and at midnight began to lay down harassing fire on enemy communication routes. Two Forward Observation parties, under Second Lieutenants Henry Counsell and Sidney RKH Reakes, co-coordinated this barrage from Observation Posts to the north of, and within, the Bois des Buttes.

Suddenly, at 1 am, the German guns opened up a furious bombardment:

The first ten minutes of the barrage consisted of heavy gas shelling. Gas masks were hurriedly adjusted and there were remarkably few casualties. Then, at 1.10 am, the enemy guns switched to High Explosive, which shrieked and blasted into the gun area for the next 65 minutes. Several German batteries were directing their efforts against the 5th Battery in an effort to destroy the guns. The telephone lines to the OPs were soon severed. In these severely testing circumstances, Captain Massey personally took control of the firing of the Battery whilst the Gun Position Officer, Lieutenant JE Large, and Second Lieutenant CA Button commanded the Sections. To continue to serve the guns indefinitely during such a terrific barrage was a physical impossibility for any man. Realising this, Captain Massey organized a system of reliefs with two gunners and one NCO manning each gun at any one time. The remainder took cover until their turn came around to take their places at the guns.

Lieutenant Large and Second Lieutenant Button frequently took their places with the gunners in the reliefs, whilst Captain Massey kept moving from gun to gun and from dugout to dugout, encouraging the

Captain John Hamon Massey, OC, 5 (Gibraltar) Battery

detachments and telephonists. At 3.35 am it was 5th Battery's turn to suffer the concentrated attentions of the German guns. If the earlier counter-battery fire had been frightening, the redoubled hammer blows of the massed German batteries was truly terrifying. Casualties, killed and wounded, increased. Number 4 gun was put out of action by shell splinters. The Number 3 gun had a very lucky escape when a German shell exploded on the edge of the ammunition pit. Splinters from this shell wounded several of the detachment, including Lieutenant Large. This young officer lost most of his right foot but refused to leave his Battery in order to have it seen to at the Dressing Station.

By 5 am the British Forward Zone on 8th Division's front had been overwhelmed. Gunner Fay, of the 5th Battery wrote later from captivity concerning the fate of one of the battery's OPs: *Mr Counsell, two Trench Mortar Officers, another Gunner and myself fought with rifles from a trench. Mr Counsell was shot in the head and killed. He was very brave.*

Despite being still under fire, the 5th Battery continued to provide as much support as it could. By 6 am the sounds of heavy infantry fighting

8th Division artillery barrage map.

echoed from the right in the direction of Bois des Buttes. A little later the German artillery fire lifted clear of the 5th Battery's position and at 6.30 am large numbers of German infantry and machine-gunners hove into view, no more than 200 yards from the gun pits. Captain G Donaldson, writing in the *British Army Review* (1987), takes up the story:

> *Captain Massey ordered 'Direct Fire' in defence of the gun position before picking up a Lewis gun and personally leading the counter-attack force to the trenches beside Number 5 gun. The artillery rounds, fired at point blank range, were very effective and Captain Massey and his band pushed off to the right, intending to drive the German infantry away.*

Meanwhile the Germans had managed to turn the Battle Zone of 149 Brigade:

> *This breakthrough released more German troops into the rear of the 5th Battery Gun Position at the same time as a fresh onslaught was started from the front. Captain Massey had not returned, so Lieutenant Large, despite being wounded, assumed command. He ordered the guns to use 'Direct Fire' again and sent Lieutenant Button into the Command Post dugout to burn all*

the maps and documents. Taking the other Lewis gun, Large joined the detachment on Number 5 gun who were making a stronghold of their ammunition pit. Those Gunners with personal weapons fired their rifles from behind the sandbags whilst those who were not so fortunate continued to blaze away as best they could with the guns. As the enemy closed, Lieutenant Large eventually had to order the gunners to remove and damage their dial sights. He passed the order to guns five and six, but as he struggled to stand and shout to the other guns he was shot through the lungs and died immediately. Second Lieutenant Button joined the fight but he too was killed minutes later. When the Germans finally stormed onto the position, the fight became a bloody hand–to–hand brawl with rifle butts, bayonets, picks and spades. Of the three officers and forty-six NCOs and men of 5th Battery RFA, only five men escaped death or capture.

Gunner E Harper, who volunte to go round the gun pits Captain Massey during morning 27 May and was with when he died of wounds later day.

In a letter written by Bombardier Birley, first to the grieving mother of Captain Massey and then to the relatives of Second Lieutenant Button, the commander's fate was outlined:

The Captain and Lieutenant were with me as the Boche made for the guns and put 73 Sub-Section gun out of action. I being the No1 of the Detachment, picking up a rifle, we made for a communication trench in the rear, both Officers armed with revolvers and ammunition. Hotly pressed, the Captain made for the wood further to the rear, followed by Mr Button and myself, we were flanked on both sides by the Boche so made a fight for it.

Mr Button was shot through the heart and myself through the right breast, the same bullet struck Captain Massey above the heart. I dropped in a trench where I lay for a time then got up and

Bombardier Fred Birley, 5th Battery, taken prisoner near Bois des Buttes.

made for the Officers to see if anything could be done. Finding Mr Button dead I turned to Captain Massey, forcing some water in his mouth. Whilst doing this I made to get up and walk along with other prisoners to a Dressing Station some 17 kilometres behind the Boche line. While laying there I saw Captain Massey brought in and calling that he was put next to me on a stretcher. Now each case of wounded was inoculated and a Serjeant who came to inoculate me, I asked him if there was any possibility of Captain Massey living but he said no.

By 8 am on 27 May 1918 not a single British artillery battery in either XXXIII Brigade RFA or XLV Brigade RFA was still in action. The only gun to survive was that from the 5th Battery still in the workshops.

5th Battery, XLV Brigade RFA was awarded the distinction of the Croix de Guerre with two Palms as an official recognition of their bravery.

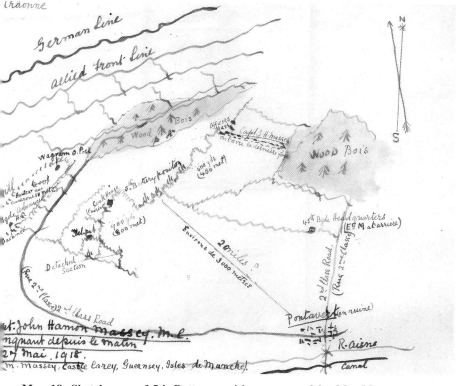

Map 18: Sketch map of 5th Battery positions prepared by Mrs Massey based on reports she received from eye-witnesses. The map was prepared for the French military authorities in a bid to help find her son.

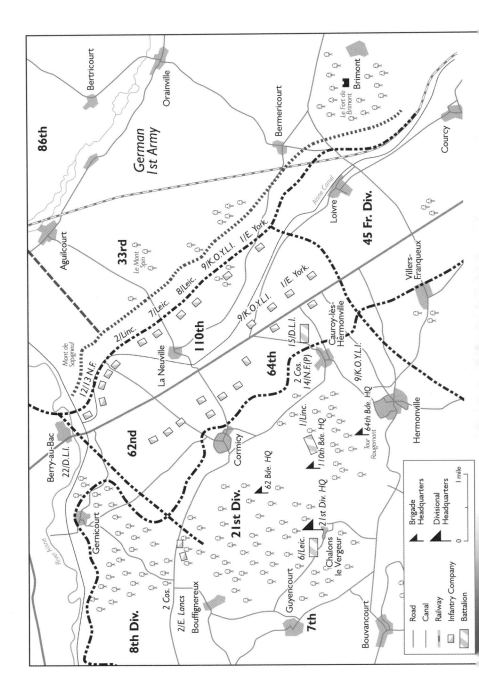

134

Chapter Four

THE DEFENCE OF THE AISNE CANAL:
The 21st Division

21st Division

The 21st Division held a front of roughly five miles south of the Aisne, running almost parallel to Route 44 – the main Laon to Reims highway. The land here was very flat and swampy, and the dominant feature was

the Aisne and Marne canal, which ran between the Forward and Battle Zones. Brigadier General Hanway R Cumming, of 110 (Leicestershire) Brigade, was far from impressed with the divisional front and the men who held the line:

The divisional front extended for a distance of 7,500 yards. 110 Brigade had a front of 2,500 yards to be held by three weak battalions, who had been filled up recently by a large proportion of young and untrained men, and there had been little time to rectify this before going into the line.

The position on the divisional front was a bad one; the Aisne Canal ran along the whole length of it and divided it into two portions, the area east of the canal and that west of it. On the flanks the forward line ran close to the canal, but in the centre it made a deep loop away from

Brigadier Hanway R Cumming.

it, the greatest distance being about 1,000 yards. The Canal itself was broad and constituted a formidable obstacle, which was enhanced by a belt of marsh about 150 yards broad, lying immediately to the east of it. The area east of the canal formed in this way an Outpost Zone for the remainder of the area West of it, but it was entirely dominated by the Boche positions - Hill 108, Mt. Sapingneul, and above all Mt. Brimont.

However, the area to the west of the canal was on the whole well prepared, having a double belt of strong points connected by a strong trench line. This position lay on the crest of a ridge overlooking the canal, with good views over No Man's Land. This potential strength

135

Major General DCM Campbell, OC, 21st Division.

was nullified, according to Cumming, because of the insufficient number of troops allotted to it.

Major General George Addison, Commander Royal Engineers, 21st Division, was even more vehement in his criticism of the weaknesses of the position held by the troops of the division, particularly the Forward Zone, which was sited to the east of the canal. Major General David 'Soarer' Campbell, GOC 21st Division, along with Addison, had complained to the French High Command about trying to fight from such a position, with a Forward Zone effectively isolated by the canal to its rear. Recommendations were made to give up this zone and concentrate on fighting behind the canal, which in itself would have been a formidable obstacle. These proposals were brushed aside by General Duchêne; the Forward Zone had to be maintained

Despite the refusal of the French to abandon the Forward Zone, Addison had implemented a number of changes to the defences of the 21st Division's front. In the three weeks leading up to the attack the number of troops occupying positions across the canal was cut back to

Trench map from May 1918, showing positions occupied by the 62 Brigade

a minimum. A considerable number of bridges over the canal were removed – allowing two per brigade, which were prepared for demolition in the event of an attack – and the trench system was reorganised into a number of strong points, served by a reduced number of communication trenches, whilst the remaining trenches were filled in or blocked. Not all of these changes had been brought about by 27 May, but these improvements helped as we shall see, to slow down the German advance in this sector.

62 Brigade

The position of the front held by 62 Brigade was the most northerly of the 21st Division. On 27 May the Forward Zone was held by two companies of the 12/13 Northumberland Fusiliers and three companies of the 2/Lincolns. The 1/Lincolns were in brigade reserve at Châlons le Vergeur. The German artillery bombardment commenced at 1 am in the sector of the 21st Division. 62 Brigade's War Diary reports that the shelling was very heavy, especially on the Battle Zone; the front line positions were practically untouched prior to the infantry assault. Until 7 am the situation of the companies across the canal was very confused, owing to the heavy gas cloud that enveloped the low lying areas of the canal. The advance of the First German Army was much more cautious than their counterparts in the Seventh Army and, as a result, 12/13 NF were still holding grimly on to the Battle Zone at 7.15 am. There are

German Army observation post at Cote/Hill 108, above the Aisne.

few details with regard to the fate of the 2/Lincolns, who appear to have been surrounded by the enemy fairly quickly, only two officers and about thirty ranks getting away.

The 1/Lincolns were in brigade reserve near Châlons le Vergeur, on top of the hilly St Auboeuf ridge. This was heavily wooded country, and the subsequent fighting in this area was to become very confused. The road to the village of Cormicy near to the Battle Zone of the 62nd Division was through a large forest. Only when encountering the area between Cormicy and Route 44 did the gradients lessen and the woods disappear. At 5.15 am the 1/Lincolns were ordered to move from their reserve position to cover the village of Cormicy. It was reported that the Northumberlands to the north were falling back and it was vital that a defensive flank was formed with a group of French Territorials, who had also moved up into support, to

Second Lieutenant AK Collins, 12/13 NF, KiA 29 May.

prevent German forces from moving into the woods. Any penetration here by enemy troops would have threatened units of the 8th Division on the Aisne. The Lincolnshire battalion managed to hold this position against a number of enemy

Private WJ Nash,
12/13 North Fus,
KiA 27 May.

Lieutenant Colonel R
Bastard, 2/Lincolns,
PoW 27 May.

assaults until 1 pm. It was not long before German troops occupied Cormicy from the south, and the depleted companies of the Lincolnshire were forced to fall back into the valleys and hills of the St Auboeuf ridge; by now both flanks were in the air. At 3 pm a line was stabilised along the Cormicy – Châlons le Vergeur road with support from the 4th South Staffordshire Regiment, part of the 25th Division.

110 Brigade

110 Brigade held the centre of the divisional front, containing a portion of the front line between Sapigneul and Brimont at the point where it ran furthest east of the Aisne Canal, some 1,500 metres. The canal 'looped' through the brigade sector, and the two companies within the battalions guarding the flanks of the Forward Zone were hemmed in between the canal and the front line trenches. Although many of the forward areas of the brigade

Captain JT Preston,
2/Lincolns, taken prisoner
at 9.30am near Cormicy
(Liddle Collection).

Trench map of Cormicy and positions held by the Leicestershire Brigade

were overlooked, further back, near Brigade Headquarters, camouflage and the dense woodland of the St Auboeuf ridge proved effective in shielding the areas of reserve and assembly from the German guns on the morning of the attack. Furthermore, the lofty heights of the ridge allowed the enemy forward areas and main lines of supply to be effectively observed in the days leading up to the attack. Despite this, brigade observers picked up very few signs of the forthcoming attack, as the Brigade War Diary makes clear:

> *The general atmosphere of the sector was absolutely calm prior to 27 May. Shelling was almost negligible and Trench Mortaring slight and practically confined to one small area. Hardly any registration took place. On the 25th the enemy line was raided by two parties of the 7th Battalion Leicestershire Regiment, but the front line was found empty and the second line of trench too strongly wired to be approached. Enemy patrols had ceased their activity as soon as they had found our own aggressive. Excessive movement in the back areas (including the laying of cables and air lines on the 26th) and determination to avoid identification, were thus the only two normal indications of an offensive.*

8/Leicesters held the right sub-sector with the 7/Leicesters on the left with the 6th battalion in brigade reserve. One company of the 6/Leicesters was brought forward to reinforce the 7/Leicesters in the line as soon as it became evident that an attack was imminent. The nucleus parties of the 7th and 8th battalions, who were at the transport lines, were organised into a company and ordered to a position of readiness, east of the Cauroy-Cormicy road, by 1 am.

Brigadier General Cumming witnessed the opening bombardment on his sector:

The indications were so slight and everything was so calm that the chance of an attack seemed very small to the Brigadier's mind, but the information proved incorrect. No doubt could possibly be entertained after the beginning of the opening bombardment at 1am on the 27 May that it was the prelude to a very heavy attack. This bombardment was extremely intense, with all calibres, shrapnel, high explosive, and gas being used. Everything was wrapped in fog until after 8 am and it was quite impossible to see anything from either the forward OPs or from those in the St. Auboeuf ridge

Lance Corporal W arrow, 7/Leicesters.

Communication with the front line battalions proved difficult, the telephone cables had not been buried and after the commencement of the bombardment all telephonic activity forward of Brigade Headquarters ceased. During the early hours of the attack messages were received from the front line battalions by runner, which merely detailed the heavy shelling and the extremely limited visibility.

Lance Corporal William Farrow's, of the 7/Leicesters, experience was typical of men stationed in the front line trenches at this stage of the battle:

At about 3 am they opened fire on our trenches with trench mortars and whizz bangs, and kept up a murderous rain of projectiles until 5 am, when the barrage lifted, and we found that it was followed by a horde of German infantry. They were all over the place, here, there and everywhere, front, sides and rear, and we were confronted whichever way we turned by the muzzles of rifles and the demand that we put our hands up. This we were obliged to do and then we were directed which way to take to get out of our own barrage, and later placed in charge of armed guards who conducted us through the German lines.

Private FC Clark (back row centre), 7/Leicesters, KiA 27 May.

At 7.15 am the 7/Leicesters reported that the enemy had captured La Neuville (just east of the canal in the 110th's Forward Zone) and were pressing down the road to Cormicy. Shortly after, a message mentioned enemy patrols over the canal to the west that were attacking the brigade's Battle Zone. This information troubled Cumming, as he had received no reports of a massed enemy infantry attack east of the canal, furthermore it was believed that the strongpoints in the Battle Zone would be able to deflect any frontal assault for a considerable period of time:

> It was evident from the initial stages that something extraordinary had occurred, and that from some cause or other the weight of the attack was coming from the North, and this indeed proved to be the case. The forward area East of the Canal, although attacked in the front, was also turned and attacked round its left flank, with the result that the whole of the garrison was surrounded and cut off before they had a chance to retire across the Canal.

This proved to be a very serious loss as a third of the Brigade's strength had thus disappeared. The enemy had been able to reach the canal very quickly and work along it to get behind the Leicesters' lines, as a result there was no possibility of retreat in fairly orderly stages, owning to the virtual annihilation of the companies east of the canal. It proved difficult to estimate the exact time of the attack, but it was presumed

A street fighting scene next to the church in Cormicy by German artist Georg Schobel.

that it started between 3 am and 4 am. Certainly by 8 am those companies of 110 Brigade in the Forward Zone were stranded and engulfed by the enemy.

Reginald Kiernan, a private in the reserve company of 7/Leicesters, recalls being ordered forward after 6 am through a number of shallow trenches, camouflaged partially by thick undergrowth, and coming under intense shellfire:

The officer and the corporal with two men went through the shrubbery. Looking through it I could see a big 'route nationale'. There were hundreds of our fellows running along it, like a football crowd running for the trams. Jerry's machine guns were going and they were dropping a score at a time and lying in heaps. From the 'Labyrinth' we fell back down a woody lane. There was shelling at all points. We could see Jerries now, coming over the fields, through the wire and camouflage. They looked like harvesters or men mowing. We fired at them for a short time, and then fell back. Their shells covered the fields in front of them, and fell always a bit nearer to us.

We defiled through a wood, crossed an open space, and lined the edge of another wood. Jerry came out of the wood we had left in ones and twos, but dodged back when we fired at him. The range was 500 yards. There was now no sign of any movement in the wood.

From Kiernan's testimony the battalions manning the front line had clearly been severely damaged by shellfire and enemy machine guns. This was no orderly retreat and, according to Cumming, was almost wholly due to the German infantry having broken through to the north. Cumming claims that the 50th and 8th Divisions were unable to prevent the enemy reaching the Aisne and seizing the bridges over it, and, *By reason of these developments, the left flank of the 21st Division became uncovered and remained so for the rest of the operation.* As a result of this, many of the units east of the canal, who had been able to hold their ground against the frontal attack, found that their left flank was turned and were enveloped along the line of the canal. This set a pattern, according to Cumming, for the next few days:

The enemy pressed the advantage which was thus obtained during the remaining days of the withdrawal, but was unable to break the line or the cohesion with the 45th French Division. He was continually turning the left flank, which remained 'en l'air' and thus forcing the Division to pivot on the right flank by continually throwing back the left, until troops could be brought up to fill the gap.

By 8 am the enemy was across the canal and began to attack the Battle Zone of 110 Brigade. German infantry began to overcome the double belt of strong points held by the 8th and 6/Leicesters.

Lieutenant Alfred Halkyard of the 8/Leicesters was particularly impressed with the German infantry's penetration in the sector held by his battalion:

The use made by the enemy of his infiltration method in this attack was most noticeable on the front under my own observation. Small parties under a junior NCO or senior soldier were most persistent in working forward in dead ground or down communication trenches (of which all could not be blocked and held) and any part of the front where the enemy met with serious opposition was subsequently left alone.

The forward Companies were quickly overrun and the enemy was crossing and passing round the flanks of the marsh soon after 6 am. The strong points, however, East of the Reims – Berry-au-Bac Road and supporting platoons along the road itself, held out for some time and it was not until 10 am that the enemy's infiltration and outflanking methods and use of the dead ground and unoccupied communication trenches caused these posts to become untenable.

It was not long before battalion headquarters of the 8/Leicesters at Vauban fell, despite the efforts of one company of the 7/Leicesters and one of the 21st Battalion Machine Gun Corps, who had been called upon to shore up resistance in the sector. The Brigade War Diary concluded that, at 10 am, *All strong points between Route 44 and the canal had been cut off, though not all had been overcome.* The command post, Tenaille de Guise, to the south east of Cormicy, had to be taken twice by enemy forces before resistance was finally overcome. Some of the fighting here was particularly gruesome. Sergeant Harold Betts of 8/Leicesters testified after the war to the treatment meted out to troops who surrendered:

Sergeant H Betts 8/Leicesters, taken prisoner 27 May.

On the day of my capture I saw some of our wounded, about five of them, who had been caught by one shell, killed by Germans, who bayoneted them. These men were from the same regiment as mine, but a different battalion. I also saw a platoon of Northumberland Fusiliers lined up on a parapet before a German Flammenwerfer – fifteen of them were killed. There was no German officer there, it was done by the German soldiers on their own. When my party came up in charge of a German officer, a lieutenant, he stopped it, that is, the German soldiers. Four or five of them stopped when they saw him.

Captured British troops at Amifontaine holding camp. (Liddle Collection)

During the course of the afternoon a period of consolidation ensued as German reserves were brought forward. Captain David Kelly, the intelligence officer on the staff of 110 Brigade, recalls the scene:

> *When the fog lifted we could see from the top of St. Auboeuf ridge what was going on, and later could observe a stream of enemy reinforcements coming up a wood, the 'Bois Allonge', close to my observation post, and emerging from thence in small parties to renew their attacks.*

Captain David Kelly, intelligence officer on the staff of 110 Brigade. After the war he became a distinguished diplomat.

145

Private Albert McNaughton, 6/Leicesters, killed in the opening hours of the attack.

146

Espin overlooked the trenches of 64 Brigade.

By the early evening 110 Brigade had fallen back further, in line with the two other brigades of the 21st Division, along the Cormicy-Cauroy road. The remnants of 62 Brigade held on to Cormicy village, and 64 Brigade guarded the outskirts of Cauroy, in touch with the French 45th Division on their right.

64 Brigade

64 Brigade held a front of just over a mile and a quarter, with the right just north of the village of Loivre and the left on the Boyau Godat. On the right of the brigade was the French 45th Division (the front line held by the 3rd Zouaves) and on the left 110 Brigade. The line of outposts east of the canal was lightly held by two companies from each of the 1st East Yorkshire and the 9th King's Own Yorkshire Light Infantry (KOYLI). There were two companies placed in the main line of resistance, the Battle Zone, which lay to the west of the Marne – Aisne Canal; one company was placed in reserve. The reserve battalion, 15 Durhams, was at Châlons le Vergeur, close to divisional Headquarters. 64 Brigade held the extreme eastern sub-sector of IX Corps and, for this reason, the brigade also had three companies of the 14 Northumberland Fusiliers (Pioneers) and 126 and 98 Field Companies RE placed under its tactical command. The original defence scheme of the French was adopted. For a raid or small-scale attack the picquet lines were to be closed and a defence was to be organised on the Outpost Zone. In the event of an attack on a large scale, those companies to the east of the canal were to withdraw over the canal, blowing up the bridges as they went, and then they were to join those companies manning the line of redoubts in the Battle Zone.

Brigadier General Hugh Headlam was less than impressed with the front occupied by his brigade. He felt that the decision taken by the

French commander, who had occupied this sector prior to the arrival of the 21st Division, was 'ludicrous', as the Outpost Zone was *practically a swamp and only had three or four crossing places*. As a result, the British troops across the canal were 'marooned'. He had recommended to his superior, Major General Campbell, that the companies occupying the Forward Zone be withdrawn. Campbell passed on this request via Corps to the French; General Duchêne refused. Headlam felt that this decision had grave consequences:

> *If the three forward companies had been withdrawn, a barrage could have been put down on the crossing places over the canal and the three companies could have been saved and helped to strengthen the Battle Zone: as it was, they were just blotted out and overrun, and the Germans were able to cross.*

News of the impending German attack came late to 64 Brigade. A message was received from the French troops to the right at 9 pm on the evening of 26 May that there were signs of an imminent German assault. According to the War Diary of 9 KOYLI, German preparations had been apparent for two or three days. Ammunition dumps were being built and new trenches dug, wire had been cleared and large bodies of troops were seen mustering in the rear, but *Beyond this, however, the general, if somewhat ominous, quietude which reigned disarmed suspicion.* At 9.30 pm a message arrived at Brigade Headquarters which finally confirmed that the German attack was to take place at 1 am. In some instances the troops in the outpost zone only received news of this attack at 11 pm. At 12.30 am instructions were issued to destroy a number of bridges over the canal as soon as the enemy attacked - a mere thirty minutes before the bombardment commenced. It seems doubtful if any of the bridges were destroyed, as 9/KOYLI's War Diary makes clear:

> *It is probable that many planks were left which the Germans used to make a footbridge. It would have been better for an RE party to have been at all the crossings to see that the task was satisfactorily completed.*

The German bombardment opened up precisely on time as predicted. *An Account of the Part Taken by the 64th Infantry Brigade in the Operations of 27 May to the 30 May*, written by Captain Lancelot Spicer (the Brigade Major), provides the following report of the barrage:

Captain L D Spicer, Brigade Major, 64 Brigade.

Heavy bombardment opened along the whole front, a large amount of gas being mixed with HE. The gas used was of several kinds, but there appeared to be a large proportion of Yellow Cross [mustard gas]. It was impossible to tell the exact frontage of the bombardment but judging from the sound alone, it seemed to be heavier to the North than to the South.

The gas shelling was much heavier in the Battle Zone than on the trenches east of the canal. Box respirators were put on everywhere and worn until the German infantry attack developed. This was a particular cause for concern, which prompted the author of 9 KOYLI War Diary – Major Harry Greenwood VC – to comment that,

The result was that our men were fatigued, sore about the face and without breakfast to commence a long day's battle. The Germans probably had breakfast in comfort. It is a matter for consideration for Superior Commanders whether we should not use gas in our counter-preparations and so let our men start on fair terms with the Germans.

Major Harry Greenwood, adjutant 9 KOYLI; he later won the VC for his actions at Ovillers, 24 October.

It would appear that the telephone wires were cut very early in the bombardment. As a result there was little communication with the companies holding the ground east of the canal; and due to the clouds of gas and smoke hovering over the battlefield, it proved difficult to tell when the German infantry advance began in this sector. Spicer reported that very heavy drumfire was heard for about thirty seconds at 3.45 am and this heralded the beginning of the attack. The War Diary of 9/KOYLI reports this action much earlier, at just after 3 am. It was not until 5 am that news of events east of the canal reached battalion and Brigade Headquarters. Lieutenants Shaw and Holmes, who had been captured by the Germans and escaped, reported that the outposts had held for an hour or so. Advance parties of the enemy infantry were held off by both rifle and grenade fire, but the Lewis gunners had been the most successful in inflicting casualties as the enemy attempted to penetrate the wire obstacles. The trench system in this part of the front was particularly deep and once the German infantry were over the front line the fighting was to be characterised by bombing down the multitudes of communication trenches and redoubts. The infiltration tactics employed by the enemy managed to mop up any centres of resistance. Some of the redoubts adjacent to the west bank of the canal held out for a few hours, but by about 7 am most of these bastions had been surrounded and the occupants taken prisoner.

The use of the Yellow Cross gas proved devastating. Captain George Ellenberger, commanding C Company, was making his way to Wattignies Redoubt in the Battle Zone when he was caught up in the German barrage and suffered from the effects of gas. He was helped back to his dugout further in the rear by his second in command, Lieutenant J P Shaw, feeling distinctly groggy:

> *I remember going on with Shaw in a sort of nightmare. We passed my servant, Miller – I think he said he was gassed. In the dugout I remember Shaw told me that Sergeant Tilbrook was badly and probably fatally hit, but he was taken down alive. My next recollection is of finding myself with Shaw standing in the trench two or three hours later in the early morning. The Germans suddenly appeared and seemed to be around us in no time. No 'SOS' went up from the front line.*
>
> *We fired at figures advancing through the mist: one Lewis Gun, I remember, was completely driven from its position by a machine gun firing from somewhere close at hand. We were bombed from both sides, and found the French bombs, which were all we had, absolutely ineffective and outclassed. It was soon all over, and we found ourselves prisoners. Shaw, I lost, he was wounded I believe, but I hear he was brought back safely by the Germans.*

The 1/East Yorks occupied the extreme right of IX Corps on the morning of 27 May. Like 9/KOYLI, the 1/East Yorks had one of its companies stationed beyond the Aisne canal. This gave Captain Stanley Howard, Adjutant of the battalion, much concern:

> *The canal was not entirely filled with water and communication across it was by plank bridges, for it was a narrow stream. The weakness of the forward Company's position in case of attack was recognized, but according to the scheme of defence the position could not be abandoned without Army authority.*

Indeed, not long after the infantry attack at 6 am, the precarious position occupied by D Company proved its undoing. After a desperate resistance the company was captured almost en bloc. Captain Howard takes up the story:

> *For a time the enemy did not exploit their success on our*

Battalion front, but started an enveloping tactic to the left of A Company's front. Under Captain Watson it put up a good fight, but suffered heavily in casualties from mobile machine guns. Their post on the left covered a valley running at right angles to our front, and between us and the KOYLIs. Down this valley the Germans poured their strength. Seeing this was the weak point of our defence, Colonel Alexander sent Second Lieutenant Lionel G Middlebrook of the 64 Brigade Trench Mortar (Stokes) Battery, with his guns. He was lent to us for the battle, and he established

his guns in A Company's line, and put up a most successful and destructive barrage with his guns. In a short space of time he fired 100 rounds (his whole store) and this damped the enemy's enthusiasm for an hour or so. Middlebrook was awarded the Military Cross for the way he kept the enemy back and his persistent enthusiasm was an example to us all.

Lieutenant Colonel AJ McCulloch, CO 9/KOYLI.

By 9 am the main line of resistance in the Battle Zone was being threatened and a request was made by the CO of 9/KOYLI, Lieutenant Colonel Andrew McCulloch, for reinforcements. Two platoons of the 15 Durhams were despatched from brigade reserve and helped form a defensive flank on the left. This was a desperate measure, as 110 Brigade had fallen back to Centre Vauban and the Battle Zone of the KOYLI was being machine gunned from the left rear and enemy bombers were working their way along Route 44. Some of the redoubts in the Battle Zone held out for another two hours. This was the case with A Company at Jemmapes Post, who were subjected to a prolonged enemy bombardment before making two counter-attacks and driving away German infantry on their front. Nevertheless, the enemy continued to exploit weaknesses in the defence using Route 44 and penetrating the Battle Zone from the left.

Colonel McCulloch attempted to remedy this situation by advising 1/East Yorks, holding the extreme right of the British line, to throw out a defensive flank facing in a north-westerly direction to counter enemy penetration along Route 44. McCulloch also informed Lieutenant Colonel William Alexander of the East Yorks that 9/KOLYI were withdrawing battalion headquarters to Cauroy, as they were being surrounded from the left. These messages, delivered by different runners, caused confusion and Alexander took the unilateral decision to withdraw his battalion to Hermonville, south west of the Battle Zone. However, it would appear that orders for withdrawal were not communicated to the right company holding the front, which had hardly been attacked and was in close touch with the French. Headlam was furious with this decision, as a gap opened up between the KOYLIs and the East Yorks, allowing the Germans to make further inroads into 64 Brigade's Battle Zone. Writing to Sir James Edmonds in the mid 1930s, Headlam explained:

> The 1/East Yorks were not withdrawn by my order. The moment I heard of this withdrawal I sent my Brigade Major (Captain Spicer) to tell East Yorks to go back and form a defensive flank on its left. The battalion started back, but it was then too late for it to act as I had ordered. The CO left for England a few days later.

By early afternoon the resistance of 9/KOYLI in the redoubts of the Battle Zone had been overcome. This had been accomplished in the main by the enemy troops waging a successful bombing war in the deep trenches of the remaining strongpoints. By 3.30 pm, the few survivors from the KOYLIs forward companies joined with the companies of 15/Durhams and 14 Northumberland Fusiliers (Pioneers)

Cauroy trench map.

9 KOYLI · Avanncee de Cauroy · Cauroy · 15/DLI · Chalons Le Vergeur · 8/Leicesters · Centre Vauban

ttacks · German Infantry

Defence of Cauroy by 15/DLI.

in defence of Cauroy and Hermonville. This proved to be a largely successful manoeuvre, as the line held until the early hours of the following morning:

> *To get a better field of fire, the CO moved this force to the shallow trench line immediately in front of the farm one mile N E of Hermonville and half a mile south of Cauroy, defending either side of the Rabassa Ravine. We were joined later by 16 OR of the 15th Durhams under Captain Clark, who prolonged the line to the south and gained touch with the 3rd Zouaves on our right. Our detachment from this position gained good targets at the enemy coming into the Avanchée de Cauroy and assisted the 15 Durhams in repelling a grenade attack directed through Cauroy and up Beau Séjour communication trench. This went on till dark.*

As well as Brigadier General Headlam's vociferous denunciation of General Hamilton-Gordon's role as commander of IX Corps, he was also specific in his complaints relating to the performance of the 21st Division on 27 May. Headlam maintained that communication and liaison between the 21st Division and Brigade Headquarters was poor:

Captain A N Clark DSO MC, 15/DLI, he won his MC for his actions on 27 May, when he preserved his company intact as a fighting unit and put up a firm resistance.

> *I was always completely in the dark as to what was going on, and only realised the extent of the German success when I saw about a five mile frontage of the German army advancing south on the morning of 28 May.*

Furthermore, he was also concerned about the lack of artillery support given to the front line infantry battalions:

153

There was none at all on the 28th when the most glorious targets were available from Luthernay and Trigny - and none on the 27th after 10 am - when masses of Germans were advancing on Cauroy. Incidentally it was the same in the great March offensive, retiring infantry never got any artillery support. The guns were either knocked out, or got back miles themselves.

Lieutenant Colonel McCulloch (9/KOYLI) was also anxious about the lack of protection given to the infantry by the gunners. Artillery fire, he claimed, was so weak as to be 'almost non existent' and it provided 'no help to the morale of our infantry'. McCulloch also produced a report for the Official Historian in 1934, in an attempt to explain the reasons for the failure of IX Corps on 27 May. He felt that it would be a mistake for the official account to make out the defence of IX Corps a good one. He felt that, 'It was distinctly poor, more feeble than the Somme defence in March, or the Lys defence in April.'

He was also more specific in relation to his own battalion, 9/KOYLI:

The question arises, why did the defence of 9/KOYLI hold up the Germans so short a time? (On our left the British effort was even poorer) – two hours at the position held by the forward company and six hours at the position held by the rear companies.

In answering this question, McCulloch, mentions similar reasons given by other officers from the 50th and 8th Divisions: the weakness of the infantry battalions, filled with inexperienced recruits knowing little about trench warfare and even less about open warfare; the fact IX Corps had fought protracted battles in March and April; and that the front held by many battalions was excessive. However, he also praised the tactical acumen of the enemy forces. He noted that as soon as the Germans were held up by a post, they worked their way up communication trenches found not to be held, and attacked many of the redoubts from behind, 'which they bombed and captured at leisure'. The German airforce supported these attacks: 'The sky was thick with German aircraft. On the 27th and 28th May, ours were not to be seen.' McCulloch found no problems with the neighbouring brigade to the south:

The Zouaves (45th Division) on my right fought well. On the evening of the 27th I visited their nearest post: six men under a Corporal. I asked him if he meant to hold his ground unless told to go. He replied, 'Moi. Je suis zouave. Je ne bouge pas.'

Captain Spicer's report also provides details of German tactical
154

effectiveness. One of the innovative features of the German preliminary bombardment was the concentrated use of trench mortars prior to the infantry attack; and these mortar teams were equally effective following up and providing close support to the infiltrating infantry. Furthermore, the Germans made great use of 'white smoke or mist cloud (as in the previous attacks of March and April)', which cut off visual communication. The enemy made good use of the maze of trenches by bombing down them rather than attacking over the open. Many of the small scale battles fought in the labyrinthine Battle Zone were characterised by grenade lobbing on both sides. In many instances the Germans had the upper hand. According to the War Diary of 9/KOYLI the reason for this was:

> *Our men were not as proficient in a grenade fight as men of the Battalion a year ago, owing to the fact the grenade fighting has been relegated to a secondary position during the training of the last six months.*

However, despite this, the War Diary points out that hand grenade fights 'were carried out in a courageous and determined manner against superior forces'.

Unlike the artillery of the 8th and 50th Divisions, XCIV and XCV RFA Brigades of the 21st Division did not suffer as heavily. The main reason for this was that the battery positions were located further to the rear and there was no topographical impediment, like the Aisne, to prevent their withdrawal. By the late morning, orders were issued by Division for the guns to be extricated from their forward positions and to be brought back to the St. Aubouef Ridge. On the whole this was successfully achieved, apart from the loss of five guns from B Battery of XCV Brigade. B Battery had been stationed on the extreme left of the front and the guns were captured by enemy troops breaking through 8th Division's front to the north. As a result of this early retirement by the gunners, a number of post action reports were critical of the lack of support given to the front line troops in this sector. McCulloch complained that artillery support was 'so weak as to be almost non existent. It gave no help to the

Captain FA Marsden, 9/KOYLI, taken prisoner 27 May, seen here in Karlsruhe PoW camp, June 1918.

morale of the infantry.' Despite this, the artillery's early retirement enabled the guns from the 21st Division to be brought into action on subsequent days, unlike the divisional artillery to the north of the Aisne that had all fallen into enemy hands by the end of the first day.

155

Private TS Robinson, 1/East Yorks, KiA 28 May.

By 9.30 am all along the front occupied by the Sixth Army, west of Californie Plateau and the sector occupied by the 8th and 50th Divisions of the British Army, the enemy had broken through to the Aisne. At first it seemed that there remained the possibility of delaying the advance across the canal and river by destroying the bridges. In some sectors this was accomplished, but reports from the front that filtered back to General Duchêne's headquarters by 11.15 am stated that a number of bridges had already been taken by them. This left no doubt that the enemy's advance could not be contained short of the Rear Zone (Green Line), to the south of the Aisne. A new phase of the battle was about to begin.

21st Division sector from a French map

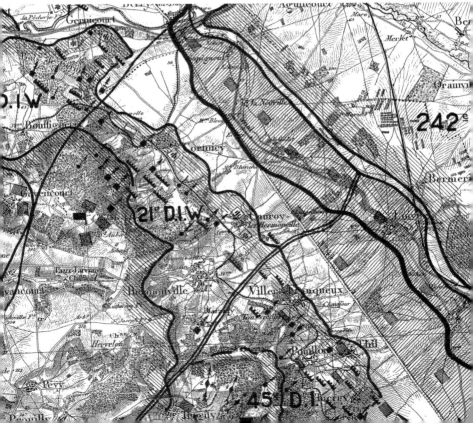

Chapter Five

REARGUARD ACTIONS:
AFTERNOON OF 27 MAY - 6 JUNE

With the rupture of the allied Forward and Battle Zones on the morning of 27 May and the advance of the Germany army to the banks of the Aisne, the battle moved into the next stage. The defensive positions of the British and French armies on the Chemin des Dames had been obliterated in less than ten hours by the enemy artillery, and those troops lucky enough not to be killed in the preliminary bombardment were taken prisoner en masse. After the leading columns of the German army had negotiated the Aisne, the battle became one of pursuit in the open country that lay to the south.

By midday on 27 May almost all the British Forward and Battle Zones of IX Corps had fallen to the Germans. This was particularly the case with the positions occupied by the 8th and 50th Divisions, where the enemy in these sectors had penetrated to the Aisne and in some

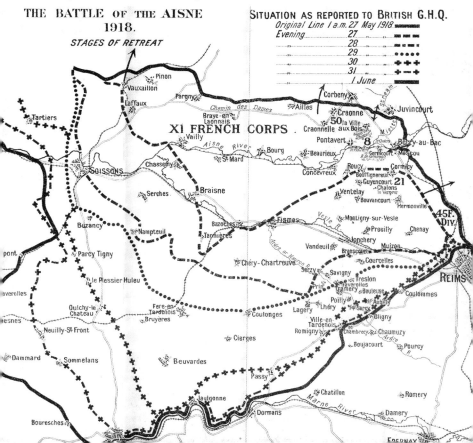

8 Siege Battery on the road towards Fismes, 27 May. Bombardier JA Toy sits next to the left wheel.

instances was already across the river and canal by the early afternoon. Isolated pockets of resistance still held out in the Battle Zone occupied by the 21st Division. Almost all the divisional artillery north of the Aisne had either been captured by the enemy or had been destroyed.

South of the Aisne stood the rudimentary fortifications of the Rear Zone (Green Line), which had been allotted to the 25th Division for defence. However, the German advance had been so rapid that the 25th Division, stationed south of this zone in the Army reserve, had not been able to reconnoitre the ground of the zone before being called upon as reinforcements. On being ordered north on the evening of 26 May, the 25th Division moved to the Aisne and was effectively fed piecemeal into the battle during the course of the next day. There the division joined up with the depleted remnants of the 8th, 21st and 50th Divisions, which had fallen back from the heights of the Chemin des Dames and positions along the Aisne and the Aisne canal. Despite the often heroic resistance of these men, intermingled with the 25th Division, the progress of the German offensive proved irresistible in moving south of the river and attacking the Rear Zone. By the early afternoon of 27 May, the Forward and Battle Zones of the positions held by the 8th and 50th Divisions had completely disintegrated.

The battle moved into its next phase. Thus commenced a general pattern of open warfare, which continued for the rest of the day's fighting and effectively lasted until the end of the battle on 6 June. Authority was maintained by the officer – and in many instances by the

NCO – on the spot. Sidney Rogerson observed: *Time after time the situation was saved by the gallantry and resource of some officer or man whose deeds have gone unheard of and unrecognised.*

27 May: The Afternoon

Towards noon on the morning of the attack a lull occurred in the fighting. The German forward divisions having overwhelmed the 8th and 50th Divisions Outpost and Battle Zones had to regroup before a passage over the Aisne river and canal was attempted. The guns of the 8th and 50th Divisions had been either captured or destroyed, along with a sizeable proportion of the artillery of the 25th Division. The CX and CXII RFA Brigades of the 25th Division had been ordered forward during the late evening of the 26 May, and had come under the command of the 8th and 21st Divisions. This proved to be a costly mistake. 110 Brigade had moved into position at Bois de Gernicourt, along the low ground south of the Aisne. A number of batteries were lost during the enemy's preliminary bombardment, and as the Battle Zone of the 8th Division to the north collapsed during the early morning, the CX brigade found itself without infantry protection. By midday the two brigades had lost fourteen guns and four howitzers.

For the rest of the day those units of the 25th Division, along with the remnants of the 8th and 50th Divisions, attempting to man the Rear Zone lacked any form of coherent artillery support. Added to this was the fact that the Germans were able to move into position for the assault across the Aisne almost unopposed. Sidney Rogerson noted the German build up for this renewed attack:

The Aisne and its attendant canal glittered like silver ribbons in the sun, but in the vacated trench area beyond hung a pall of haze and dust which, lifting at intervals, revealed the roads thick with marching regiments in field grey, with guns, lorries, and wagons. Above, like great unwinking eyes, rode observation balloons, towed along by motor transport.

Captain Veitch, of 8/DLI, watching from a position along the canal bank, observed a similar scene:

I saw a German artillery column cross the fields from Chaudardes moving at a 'walk march' towards Maizy. It seemed to be horsed with ponies. Further back a German battery wheeled into a field facing towards Concevreux. Next I saw another column away in the distance coming from the direction of

Beaurieux and also moving towards Maizy. When I ordered the NCO to open fire at the nearer column he lifted the magazine from his gun, turned it over and said 'That is all the ammunition we have left. We will need it if they try to cross here.'

Rogerson maintained that on no other occasion in the Great War did the Germans so rapidly follow up their assault; German battalions were observed advancing in fours across the British trenches of the Battle

Acting Sergeant RL Isaac 3/ Worcesters. He was wounded on 27 May at Concevreux, and died the following day. (Peter Hurn)

Roucy Village, 8th Division's HQ.

Zone, in some cases even before the last defenders were overcome. This would have presented a relatively easy target for the artillery, which could have wrought havoc on the enemy infantry and artillery columns moving on the congested roads down to the Aisne. Furthermore, a number of bridges across the river at Pontavert, Concevreux, and Maizy had not been destroyed in time. Consequently the advanced columns of the German infantry had seized these vital passages over the Aisne, and many of the units following in the wake of the enemy's vanguard were across the river and canal without let or hindrance.

Another error in the command structure also allowed the Germans to mass so effectively on the banks of the Aisne. General Duchêne had forbidden any reserve division to be sent north of the Aisne. General Hamilton-Gordon had asked several times for permission to send forward a brigade of the 25th Division to assist the 8th and 50th Divisions during the early hours of 27 May. Finally, at 7.30 am, Duchêne relented and placed the 25th Division at Hamilton-Gordon's disposal. This was too late. By this stage in the battle the Forward Zone and a good deal of the Battle Zone north of the Aisne had fallen. Two battalions - the 8/Borders and 3/Worcesters – were despatched to defend the line between Chaudardes and Pontavert, a mile to two miles in front of the Rear Zone. However, before they arrived the enemy was reported to be in control of the two villages and neither of the two battalions crossed the Aisne.

By 10 am the 25th Division was in position, with 7 Brigade (1/Wiltshire, 10/Cheshires and 4/South Staffordshire) on the right

161

Men of 3/Worcesters, Aisne Canal.

under the command of the 21st Division, holding a line from Cormicy to Bouffignereux. 75 Brigade (11/Cheshires, 8/Borders, 2/South Lancashire) held the ground in the centre, continuing the line to Roucy, placed under the 8th Division. Finally, on the left, 74 Brigade (9/Loyal North Lancashire, 3/Worcesters, 11/Lancashire Fusiliers), placed under the authority of Major General Jackson of the 50th Division, held the line from Concevreux to near Maizy.

By the early afternoon the situation was becoming critical. A gap of about two miles had opened up on the left between 74 Brigade and the French troops on the left of the British positions. This portion of the front, from Maizy to Villers-en-Prayères, was left practically undefended. Nevertheless, direct penetration through the British front was prevented by the formation of a left defensive flank through Muscourt to the hill east of Revillon. 9/Loyals, with support from 74 Light Trench Mortar Battery, 105 Field Company R E and later the twenty-four guns of the 50th Division Lewis Gun School were all prominent in shoring up defences on the vulnerable British left.

Renewed German attacks took place all along the British line between 2 pm and 3 pm. Large bodies of enemy infantry advanced in open order along a front of roughly three miles. This mass attack was repelled in many sectors by rifle and machine gun fire alone, but sheer weight of numbers and a change in tactics allowed the German troops to force a number of gaps in the British defence. The enemy began to probe the weaker defences on the left, which led to a general retirement to the crest of the hills near Roucy – formerly the headquarters of the 8th Division. Those units, like 3/Worcesters at Concevreux, occupying bridgeheads over the Aisne found that the enemy had worked their way behind them and they were forced to retire to the higher ground to the south. Many of the heavily fortified positions prepared by the French in the woods above Roucy had to be abandoned and a new line was taken up astride the Roucy-Ventelay road. The defences here were scant but the field of fire was good. In the late afternoon the Germans attempted several attacks on the new line:

Captain F C Worster MC, 1/Worcesters, former classics master at St Paul's School. Won his MC on 27 May near Roucy, where he was subsequently mortally wounded.

> *Emerging from the wood cheering and shouting, they were quickly mown down by machine gun fire and driven back with heavy casualties. Foiled in this attempt to drive in the line by a frontal attack, the enemy now commenced an encircling movement round the right flank, at the same time bringing up trench mortars with which to bombard the front.*

As well as adapting to the situation by using infiltration from the flanks, German aerial activity also increased. Low flying planes machine gunned roads and defences and observation balloons accompanied the advance. As a result the enemy were able to observe every movement of the British troops, and guide the attacking infantry

Stormtroopers in action between Aisne and Vesle.

and direct the German artillery fire. These tactics were to be used throughout the day and the days that followed as they advanced across the Vesle towards the Marne. Sidney Rogerson was again on hand to offer his views:

> *The front would be pinned down by trench mortar fire, while small groups of infantry with light machine guns would dribble round in twos and threes; and, taking advantage of depressions in the ground and any natural cover, endeavour to turn the flanks of the position. The German Army might have favoured mass formations attacks at the Kaiser Manoeuvre or in the early days of 1914-5, but they had learnt well and truly since then, and between the Aisne and the Marne, 1918 gave us as fine an object lesson in open warfare and the use of cover as the most academic Aldershot staff-officer could have desired.*

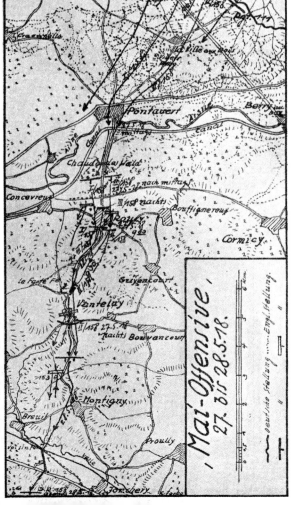

As a result of the more structured assaults by the enemy, there was an urgent need for 75 Brigade, and consequently the 25th Division, to withdraw. By the early evening, remnants of the 8th, 25th and 50th Divisions had successfully retired to the next ridge, south of Ventelay. Some units were sacrificed in this struggle. 8/Borders, covering the departure, beat off a number of German assaults before falling back through Ventelay and unintentionally linking up with the French 3rd Battalion 21st Regiment. Other battalions also held up the German advance, for example, the 11 Lancashire Fusiliers at Muscourt, where

Route taken by the German 50 ID, 27-28 May

Lance Corporal Halliwell won one of the two VCs that were awarded for actions on 27 May.

Before midnight the British line had gradually retired to new positions on the ridges west of the Ventelay-Montigny road. The left flank was well to the rear, where small groups of French troops from their Reserve were helping to fortify the gap that the Germans had opened up earlier. With the retirement of 75 Brigade it became imperative that 74 Brigade should also follow, which it did, in turn falling back to the ridge north of Montigny. Casualties had been very heavy. On the morning of the 28 May, the strength of 74 Brigade was twenty-six officers and 324 other ranks, 75 Brigade being roughly the same. Touch had been established with the French to the left, but a gap had opened on the right and connection with 7 Brigade (25th Division) had been lost. 7 Brigade had linked up with the remains of the brigades of the 21st Division, who had pivoted in a southwesterly manner, and had overlapped with French forces to the east, near Hermonville. These new positions were thinly manned and disjointed, with several gaps and little or no artillery support; for example, the 1/East Yorks, reduced to about one hundred men, held a line over a thousand yards long, linked by a chain of redoubts.

By evening on the first day the British and French divisions in the centre and left of the front had been driven back over the Aisne; and in the centre – the apex of the enemy attack – the German infantry had swept over the Rear Zone (Green Line). Other defensive positions, to the south, occupied by allied

Lance Corporal Joel Halliwell
VC, 11/Lancs Fusiliers.

Major Harold T Forster, Royal Berks attached 2/Northants. He played county cricket for Hampshire. Badly wounded in the face and body from a shell burst on 27 May near Ventelay. He died two days later and is buried in Terlincthun British Cemetery.

troops had been turned, and in a number of cases the advance had reached the Vesle. The Official History commented:

> *In the course of a summer day the enemy had crossed two, and in places three, rivers; he had driven a salient twenty-five miles wide at the base and extending nearly twelve miles into the Allied line; he had destroyed four of the divisions originally in the line, and nearly destroyed two more* (British 21st and the French 61st), besides two others (British 25th and French 157th) sent up from the reserve.

Captured British doctors at the British field hospital at Mont Notre Dame, 28 May.

The retreat of IX Corps from Vesle to Ardre.

28th May to 30th May: Forward to the Marne

The objective of the Seventh Army after the first day's tremendous progress was simply to keep advancing to the Marne. However, it was not a matter of pressing ahead regardless; the wings of the attack had to be considered. The German offensives of March and April came to a standstill due to the outer edges of the attack failing to keep up with the central push. Allied counterattacks on the flanks by fresh reserves helped to keep frontal penetration in check. It was imperative that the flanks were secured by broadening the thrust and taking strategically important French towns such as Soissons to the west and Reims to the east. Soissons fell on the evening of 28 May, Reims never did. The German advance from 27 May to the end of the month cut against the grain of the country. Interior communication lines – railways and roads – in northern France served Paris in an east-west manner, and the only railway into the salient opened up by the Germans on subsequent days ran along its western edge. In effect the advance was thrown off course, success in the south and the west was consolidated at the expense of the eastern flank.

One of the main reasons why the German advance lacked eastward penetration was due to the fact that the British and French line in the sector covering Reims had not been broken on 27 May. IX Corps, along with much of the French forces, on the morning of 28 May were in a state of considerable disarray. Enemy penetration had been greatest on the British centre and to the left, where touch had been lost with the French, but the 21st Division – with support from the 75 Brigade, 25th Division – had fallen back in good order and maintained a defensive line with the 45th Division.

The ground over which the battle was fought – as it progressed southwards to the Vesle and Ardre rivers – offered a number of elements in favour of a defensive position. The southern slopes of the Vesle ridge, free from woods and overlooking the valleys, were ideal for artillery batteries; but the guns of IX Corps had almost all been lost the previous day. Across the Vesle lay a number of irregular ridges, often wooded, with small valleys in which lay farms and settlements. This country was difficult to defend and suited the infiltration tactics of the attacker; ground was not gained by attacking frontally but by envelopment. The deeply cut wooded ravines were used as cover allowing the German infantry to outflank Allied defensive positions. Nevertheless, it was vital that this ground was heavily disputed by the Allies, as a rapid German advance up the sides of the Ardre valley would leave the enemy in possession of the strategically important

The wooded ravines with small settelements, between the Vesle and Ardre, favoured the attacker.

heights above the Marne. This would allow cover to be provided for a push to the west over the Marne and on to Paris, and the possibility of a simultaneously timed assault on Reims to the east. It was therefore of the utmost importance that the remains of the divisions defending the Aisne and the 19th Division coming from reserve should slow down the advance here.

Captain HF Stacke, in his history of the Worcestershire Regiment, vividly portrays the retreat of the British Army on 28 May and the days that followed. His record captures the nature of the fighting in the open country south of the Aisne, in scenes reminiscent of 1914:

> *Dawn came and with the dawn the German guns opened fire. Shells burst over the newly dug trenches and shrapnel bullets spattered down over the open hillside. The troops stood the ordeal grimly, holding their ground till the enemy's infantry [50th Division] advanced in long columns. German field batteries galloped forward into action and bombarded the half-made trenches at short range. The weak British battalions answered with bursts of musketry, which forced the German columns to deploy into a swarm of grey-clad skirmishers who came pressing on up the slope.*

Stacke's account does not just dwell on a few isolated heroic episodes of a particular battalion's actions; he also paints a picture of pandemonium and disarray:

> *The self sacrifice of the Lancashire Fusiliers enabled the other troops to retreat unchecked;… that retreat was a nightmare of confusion and misery. Beyond Montigny all order was lost. The little group which represented the 3rd Worcestershire was led by Major Traill along roads crowded with retreating troops, wagons*

169

and lorries. German aeroplanes came roaring close overhead, bombing the road and raking fugitives with machine guns, and German howitzers sent their shells crashing down along the route. The sides of the road became littered with dead and wounded. Lorries, either broken down or wrecked, blocked the road at several points, causing prolonged jams in the stream of retreat.

On the whole the withdrawal of the British Army towards the Vesle on 28 May, and on subsequent days towards the Marne, was a 'common sense' retreat. Many units had become detached from one another and troops from different outfits intermingled with formations from different divisions entirely; others had become so interspersed that they found themselves fighting alongside French troops. There were few instances of outright panic affecting large bodies of troops, but there were leaderless

Lieutenant John Nettleton, 2/Rifle Brigade (sitting).

groups of men found wandering around lacking direction. Brigadier General Grogan (23 Brigade) encountered one such group on 28 May:

Just south of Jonchery, on the main road to Branscourt, I met a solid mob of men, marching away from the fight quite steadily. As I had no time to deal with them, I gave orders to a junior officer to get them headed and stopped and brought up again.

Lieutenant John Nettleton, of 2/Rifle Brigade, had been in battalion reserve on 27 May, but had been ordered into the line late that night as part of a *'motley collection of about fifty men, cooks, batmen, clerks and so on from all regiments'*. The next day this group had become little more than isolated stragglers and on being attacked by superior enemy forces reacted as best they could:

This was retreat again, but it wasn't panic flight. If you get enfiladed by machine gun fire from a flank, it is common-sense to get out of the way. You can't do any good by staying, however brave you are; you just get killed.

This was not an atypical incident. Private RH Kiernan of the

British soldiers, some from the 12/13 NF, and French troops in Savigny-sur-Ardre on 28 May.

Leicestershire Regiment, part of the 21st Division, recalls his experiences:

> *We had a grand officer with us, just our platoon. We had not seen any of our company since the afternoon. There were twenty-five of us, with one Lewis gun. He had guided us all the afternoon and evening with his map. Neither he nor us knew our way... In the strong point the riflemen gave us all their ammunition, keeping only ten rounds, and we filled our drums.*

The same location 90 years later.

German machine gunners managed to turn the flank of this position and Kiernan's platoon were forced to find cover in a nearby wood:

We fell back, and heard the gun begin its short bursts... Back a long way we went and now we could not hear Ben's gun, but all was silent, and the German lights rose in the wood all around. On a hill in the middle of the forest there was the rest of the battalion. They were lining a breastwork, and peering into the dark, and shouted gladly when they saw us.

There was a semblance of order in the method of retreat recalled by both Nettleton and Kiernan, but in other parts of the line, there were displays of disorganised panic. Private William Hall, of the 2/East Lancs, recalls fleeing from a group of advancing German infantry:

They were all huge men, evidently Prussian Guards and they came forward in perfect order... It took a brief glance to take it all in; I hesitated for just a fraction, and as if some unseen force had pushed me, I broke into a run with my rifle at the hip and I dashed clean through the encircling robots. My dash carried me to the edge of a wood, a fusillade of shots followed me, but I bore a charmed life and was not hit.

Eventually Hall reached a road and fell in with a group of stragglers, who like him were similarly disorientated, *an isolated body of troops, with not the slightest semblance of a line; no artillery supports, and nobody apparently with any idea of Jerry's line of advance.* On being engaged by the enemy from the flank, panic set in and once more Hall and others found themselves taking off to what they considered the rear:

While some of the men were still hesitating, one of the men shouted that a Jerry tank was coming up on the other side of the hill and immediately there was a stampede to the cover of the woods below. I ran full tilt down the hill, and as the German tank breasted the crest, its machine gun blazing, I reached the bottom and crashed through some bushes into the cover of a wood.

In other sectors order was restored by commanding officers who led by example. At Jonchery during the early morning of 28 May, Grogan assumed command of a mixed group of

172

Private Daniel Oakley, 3/Worcesters, KiA 28 May.

men from the 25th, 50th and 8th Divisions who were heading south across the Vesle bridge;

> *He at once took steps to arrest this stream of stragglers and, having collected all available men, he formed a firing line along the Vesle, aligning the men on the railway embankment. By 10 am a strong and fairly well organised line had been established and the bridge heads well guarded. A good deal of sharp fighting took place, but up until 1 pm our line was maintained and heavy losses had been inflicted on the enemy as he attempted to attack.*

However, the troops cobbled together by Grogan were forced to retreat during the afternoon as the enemy turned the flank to the west. This was a pattern that was repeated during the rest of the day; but by nightfall Grogan had managed to form a line on the high ground (Hill 233) near Savigny, thanks to the joint efforts of a French regiment securing the left flank and a counter attack carried out by 2/Devons and the remains of the Worcesters.

Dawn on 29 May saw renewed German attacks on the Allied lines. By 11 am the positions held by Grogan's motley crew proved untenable as the German field artillery began to pound the ridge. Further retreat followed, eventually back to the Bouleuse Ridge, south of Treslon. Here fresh troops of the 19th Division were met. For the past ten days the division had been in reserve, training behind the lines in the area of the Fourth Army. The infantry battalions of the 19th Division were bussed to the front and arrived in the early morning of 29 May and were, with 2/Wilts, despatched to the area of the Bouleuse Ridge.

Major General G D 'Ma' Jefferys, GOC 19th Division.

There they encountered the tattered remnants of the units that had manned the positions along the Aisne on the morning of 27 May:

> *By this time the force under Grogan's command had become pitifully thin - a ragged army of Falstaffian dimensions. And what a collection! The General himself; his Brigade Staff Officers; Smythe, the GSO III 8th Division; Major Cope of the Devons; Colonel Moore of the 1/Sherwood Foresters, the only infantry CO of the 8th Division not already a casualty; two colonels of the 50th Division without a single man of the units they once commanded; a knot of machine gunners from the same division whose gun refused to function from a lack of water; a woeful*

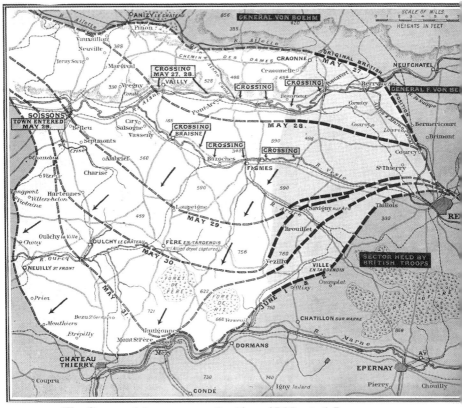

The German Advance across the Aisne, 27 May to 1 June

sprinkling of all units of the 8th and most of the 25th Division; a total perhaps of 250 - all hungry, sleepless, dirty.

Grogan rallied the troops on the slopes of Bouleuse by deliberately riding along the firing line between his men and the advancing enemy, narrowly avoiding the shells, bombs and bullets around him. According to Stacke, this reckless bravery saved the day and earned Grogan the Victoria Cross. There was no further retreat and the Bouleuse Ridge was maintained against all attacks.

The arrival of the 19th Division on the afternoon of 29 May helped to shore up defences on the Bouleuse Ridge, but the German advance had continued at a pace elsewhere. French forces were driven back some seven miles on the third day. German progress followed on 30 May, again in the centre, where German forces reached the Marne. However, on both flanks the situation stabilised. North east of Soissons, French reserves managed to stem the flow and little ground was yielded in that particular sector. Similarly around Reims, French colonial troops managed to hold out. By the evening of 30 May, the

British forces had been reduced to four divisions of composite battalions and the 19th Division had been cut back to brigade strength.

After the German breakthrough on the Aisne on 27 May, orders were issued the following day to the chiefs of staff of the attacking German Corps in simple terms: Pursuit to be continued at once. Forward to the Marne! On 28 May the German advance continued to make considerable ground; but as early as the second day of the offensive resistance on the flanks of the advance was growing. German forces were in effect being funnelled into a narrowing salient as their troops progressed southwards. Haste became imperative if the pursuit to the Marne was to be carried out in good time, as Major General von Unruh (Chief of the General Staff, Corps von Conta) observed:

> When once troops have been allowed to rest it is difficult to bring them again into rapid movement. There was no time for a corps operation order. It was a case for giving rapid individual instructions on the spot.

As the Germans pushed deeper into the Champagne region, supply became a potential hazard to the maintenance of forward movement. When French towns, such as Fismes, fell into German hands, further momentum was lost:

> There were enormous quantities of tinned food and preserves of all descriptions, which our soldiers looked on as delicacies almost unheard of. Articles of clothing, underlinen, and good English boots were seized upon with joy. Everywhere could be

A momentary pause in operations. German soldiers rest in Fismes.

heard the astonishment of our less fortunate troops, who were accustomed only to the monotonous if nourishing fare dished out by field kitchens. There were also plentiful supplies of alcohol and this was a more serious matter. There was a danger that it would slow up the momentum of the advance. The problem was to first take charge of the captured stores and organise their distribution so that every unit got its share and yet ensure that excess was avoided; and secondly to get the troops out of Fismes as quickly as possible.

German transport move towards Vesle, near the burning village of Crugny.

A similar view today.

176

The over indulgence of German troops as they fell upon the local *pinard* seems to have been a problem that affected mainly those coming up from the rear, whilst many of the attack divisions pressed on. Front line infantry units were accompanied by trench mortars but in the first couple of days of the offensive field guns were quickly brought into position to blast away any troublesome areas of Allied resistance.

By the evening of 28 May the German High Command had received a number of intelligence reports that indicated that French reserve forces stationed in the north were moving southwards to counter the German attacks. Thus Ludendorff's diversionary offensive over the Aisne was serving its purpose well. However, other reports reaching German staff officers indicated that the advance on the flanks was slow in comparison to those units in the centre, whose progress was almost unimpeded.

Captain TP Muspratt, 3/Worcesters, KiA, 29 May.

The Germans were broadly pleased with the progress that had been achieved on the first four days of the offensive. More than 50,000 prisoners had been taken, as well as about 800 field guns and thousands of machine guns. Moreover, the main aim of the attack had been accomplished, with the drawing away of French forces from the British positions further north. On the western flank, French forces to the south of Soissons were falling back; but resistance was proving stronger in the east, especially near Reims, where the French were fighting alongside the IX Corps. There were also signs, too, that lines of communication were becoming over extended and supplies of ammunition were running low.

Private E R Lazenby, 2/Wilts, KiA 31 May. Commemorated on the Soissons Memorial.

Serjeant WJ Smith, Army Veterinary Corps attached XCIV Brigade RFA. Died on 29 May of wounds sustained in an enemy air raid and is buried in Coulommiers Communal Cemetery.

31st May to 6th June: End of the Battle of the Aisne

The final days of the Aisne fighting, from 31 May to 6 June, were characterised by the German army making steady progress in the south but making little progress on the flanks. It was on the eastern flank that the remains of the IX Corps were to play an important role in defence. This sector was of vital strategic importance; Reims was an important railhead in the communications network of northern France. The acquisition of the city by German forces would help broaden out the salient that had been created since 27 May and would serve as an important supply base, whence men and material could be rushed to the front line. Both British and French forces occupied the Montagne de Reims, a series of ridges that surrounded the city from the south and east. The 19th Division, the only formation of IX Corps that was still fairly intact after the first four days of the offensive, held one of the ridges of this higher ground, the Montagne de Bligny. Any penetration by German forces along the Ardre valley and over the heights at Bligny would have allowed the enemy to establish themselves on the heights

8th Division infantry and French troops at Passy, 29 May.

of the Montagne de Reims. Once it was in German hands the fall of Reims would only be a matter of hours.

On 31 May the 19th Division was heavily shelled during the morning and attacked later in the afternoon. Although the division

suffered heavy casualties, little ground was lost. Any ground that was given up in this sector was often quickly retaken in a number of swift counter attacks by its infantry. Prominent in these actions were 2/Wilts and 9/Cheshires. Provisional battalions were formed out of the details and stragglers of the 8th, 50th, 21st and 25th Divisions and were sent forwards as reinforcements to help those British units already defending the valley of the Ardre. Furthermore, a small independent brigade, composed of three battalions of about 400 men in total and one machine gun company, was formed under the command of Brigadier General G Gater. The role of this force was to hold the south bank of the Marne from Dormans to Mareuil le Port, which it carried out successfully until relieved by the French on 11 June.

From 1 June it was clear that the German offensive was losing its momentum. The troops in the line were

Burnt out shell of tank 'Moritz' near Reims, 1 June. Blown up before it fell into enemy hands by Sergeant Leinauer and Underoffizer Sepp Dietrich. (Strasheim Collection)

facing exhaustion. Some fifteen divisions had been fighting for the best part of a week; and twelve of the fourteen reserve divisions had been used. The Allies now had thirty-three divisions committed to the battle. Operations around Reims proved disappointing. The First Army, with nine divisions, had attempted to break in on either side of Reims on 1 June, but French counter attacks were much better organised than previously. Supply became a major handicap to German progress, as Reims remained a key position without which the Seventh Army's left flank could not be adequately provisioned. British artillery from the 21st and 19th Divisions had played its part in the defence of Reims; as the Official History remarked, *The Allied artillery is said to have been definitely superior to that of the Germans in this part of the battlefield.*

From 2 to 5 June the Germans carried out only local attacks on the allied line, and the 19th Division was left in comparative peace. The last action endured by IX Corps in the Aisne battles took place on 6 June. The German objective was the hill of Bligny, 600 feet high and the key to the congested

Private SH Lang 9/North Lancs, KiA June, buried at Sissonne British Cemetery.

180

back area of Reims, just as the Mont des Cats ridge protected the rear of Ypres. The 19th Division, along with the composite brigades of the 8th, 25th and 50th Divisions, defended this area. At first light a determined attack by the German infantry wrested the summit of the hill from 9/Cheshires but an equally determined counter attack by the 4/KSLI and the survivors of the Cheshires won the heights back. The Germans did not come again while the British held this sector. General Pellé, commanding V Corps, was so pleased with the British troops under his command that he refused to release them. For another ten days 19th Division and the composite battalions of IX Corps stood guard before being relieved by the Italian 8th Division on 19 June. The British troops in the area gradually filtered back to the British sector to the north by the end of the month.

In the space of five days, from 27 May until 1 June, the German Army had advanced twenty-eight miles. At Château Thierry they were only thirty-five miles from Paris. IX Corps lost close to 30,000 men (1,298 officers and 27,240 other ranks) in the period from 27 May until 6 June. Most of the battalions who had been in the front line on 27 May ceased to exist as fighting units. Nearly 20,000 men, perhaps more, had been lost on the first day of the offensive alone, the majority now prisoners of war. The British divisions committed to the battle had fought a number of staunch rearguard actions during the retreat to the Marne, on the Bouleuse Ridge for example, but none more so than in helping to prevent the German Seventh and First Armies from taking

The view to the east of Mont Bligny, showing the exposure of the ridge. (James Pitt)

Captain John Edgar Clark MC, 9/Cheshires. He won a MC for his actions in leading the attack on Mont Bligny, 6 June.

Reims. In fact the Montagne de Reims was to be defended again by British forces in July 1918, this time by XXII Corps, who had taken over from Italian troops. It was in this sector that the 21st Division and subsequently the 19th Division maintained contact with French forces on their right flank, stopping any German breakthrough to the east. As a result the German High Command was forced into turning their consideration to following up the Aisne battle with an attempt to break French lines in the west on the Matz River, with the launching of the ill fated *Operation Gneisenau.*

In the end the German offensives petered out due not only to tactical and strategic errors – as well as the strengthening resistance of the Allies – but also because of problems with logistics. The failure of the Germans to take the strategically important city of Reims proved a costly mistake. The German Army of 1918 relied heavily on the railway and horses for mobility; they lacked the motorised columns of the BEF. Supply became a serious problem once the distance between the railhead and the front line was forty miles or more. If this gap could not be narrowed, shortages of ammunition and food became a major concern, bringing offensives to a premature halt. It also became easier for the defenders; as they retreated they fell back on their own railheads, easing their own supply problems. The final word can be left with Major General AD von Unruh:

> *Ammunition was running short and the problem of supply, in view of the large demands, became more and more difficult. It became*

all too clear that actions so stubbornly contested and involving us in such formidable losses would never enable us to capture Paris. In truth the brilliant offensive had petered out.

Nevertheless, the benchmark for tactical surprise had been set on the Aisne in May. The innovative measures that were carried out prior to 27 May to conceal an attacking force that comprised some thirty divisions and over 1,000 artillery batteries had been astonishing. The legacy of the Aisne battle was felt beyond the Western Front of 1918. Major General Hubert Essame, a brigade commander in the Second World War, observed:

The technique now to be demonstrated in its highest perfection by the Germans [on the Aisne] *was to set the pattern for most of the coming offensives of the war and to continue to be employed in World War Two on the Russian Front and finally, with remarkable initial success, in the Ardennes in December 1944.*

On 8 August, at Amiens, the British Army advanced eight miles and took 18,000 prisoners by the end of the day. To Ludendorff this

Kaiser decorates German soldiers for their success in the Aisne Battle.

represented the black day for the Germans in the war. The momentum of the BEF's attack was due in part to its mobile arm; the use of whippet tanks and two cavalry divisions. On 27 May, with far fewer tanks, the Germans advanced some fifteen miles, opening up a salient some twenty-five miles wide and took in the region of 25,000 prisoners. The tempo of this attack had been maintained by attacking infantry who were trained to use their initiative and exploit any gaps in the enemy's defences. Such a virtuoso display of tactical nous caused General Essame to remark:

> *Here, twenty years before it became a household word, in spirit at any rate, was the essence of Blitzkrieg.*

GENERAL ADVICE FOR TOURERS

The Department of the Aisne lies between Picardy and Champagne, approximately 120 kilometres north east of Paris. For those arriving via Calais, just over 220 kilometres to the north west, it is easily accessible thanks to the A26 motorway. With a Centre Parcs on Lac d'Ailette, the Golf de l'Ailette course and tours of the wineries of the nearby Champagne area, there is plenty to entertain all the family.

Whilst the Chemin des Dames and the Aisne valley are increasingly popular destinations for British visitors, there is not a large established British presence there. Accommodation, attractions and facilities are generally French owned so an at least a rudimentary grasp of the language is a definite advantage.

The Aisne battlefield is in a triangular area of land with Laon at the apex, Soissons to the south west and Reims further away, to the south east. The region is still largely rural. Accommodation is scattered and not every village has shops, a petrol station or places to eat and ones that are found may only be open at limited times. Some forward planning is therefore recommended. Up to date details of accommodation and other useful information are readily available on the internet. The following websites provide general tourist advice:

- www.evasion-aisne.com: the website of the Comité Départemental du Tourisme de l'Aisne: links to online sites to book accommodation, including Gîtes de France and Centre Parcs.
- www.aisne.com: the website of the Conseil Général de l'Aisne.
- www.tourisme-laon.fr: the Laon Tourist Office website.
- www.soissons-tourisme.fr: the Soissons Tourist Office website.

Specific tips and advice on visiting the battlefields can be found on a number of web sites, such as the Western Front Association (www.westernfrontassociation.com), the Great War Forum (www.1914-1918.invisionzone.com) and the Long Long Trail (www.1914-1918.net). They include the facility to ask questions online that usually provides very helpful responses. The much improved website of the Commonwealth War Graves Commission (www.cwgc.org) provides a wealth of information about burials by name, regiment and date.

For a more local focus, the Chemin des Dames website,

www.chemindesdames.fr, includes a virtual memorial to those who fell in the area as well as a guide to British, French and German cemeteries. Also recommended, for French speakers, is Gil Alcaix's blog, www.dictionnaireduchemindesdames.blogspot.co.uk/,

General Facilities

Looking at the villages to the south of the Aisne:

- Cormicy has a post office, supermarket, petrol station, newsagent/tobacconist, bakery and take away.
- Hermonville has a post office, bakers, pizza restaurant / take away, a small grocers that also sells gas bottles and a garage, but with no fuel pumps.
- Berry-au-Bac has a baker, a bar/tobacconist, the Restaurant de la Mairie, the Cote 108 Restaurant and a motel, Hotel des Nations.

Further afield Guignicourt is a large village with a supermarket and petrol station.

Eating Out

Tripadvisor is a useful source of information on restaurants in the area. It is best to confirm in advance that they are open on the day you wish to visit.

- La Musette is a restaurant and bar serving pizza, which is conveniently situated on the D1044 / D89 crossroads, next to La Ville-aux-Bois British Cemetery.
- On the Chemin Des Dames itself, the Caverne du Dragon has a small café and shop selling books and medals.
- In Vailly-sur-Aisne, the welcoming Pizzeria San Marino serves good pizzas and pasta dishes.
- L'Albatros restaurant at the Hôtel Restaurant du Golf de l'Ailette offers more formal seasonal menus in a tranquil lakeside setting.

Accommodation

It is recommended that you find accommodation in the villages along the Aisne valley or in Laon or Soissons.

We have enjoyed staying at the Hôtel Restaurant du Golf de l'Ailette, where most rooms have balconies overlooking the lake. The staff are friendly and helpful. It has an outdoor pool.

Centre Parcs is just a few kilometres further round the lake and may appeal to families with younger children. Day passes to Centre Parcs' Aqua Mundo water world are available for those staying elsewhere.

Maps

The 1918 Battle of the Aisne took place over a wide area. The British front line on 27 May 1918 extended for twelve miles, from the sloping ground near Craonnelle, not far from Craonne, through Berry-au-Bac to Bermericourt. In the following days the British fell back almost twenty miles, due south towards the Marne.

IGN, the French equivalent of the Ordnance Survey, offer maps in a variety of scales covering the area. IGN Carte de Promenade Maps (1:100,000) are excellent for hiking and bicycling as well as driving. IGN 09 Paris, Laon 1:100,000, covers all the battleground (apart from the village of Marfaux).

IGN Carte de Randonnee Maps (1:25,000) are precisely detailed and highly recommended for walkers. The relevant ones are:

- Carte IGN Craonne - IGN 2711E
- Carte IGN Beaurieux - IGN 2711O
- Carte IGN Gueux - IGN 2712E
- Carte IGN Sissonne - IGN 2710E

The iPhiGéNie app offers digital maps of France with GPS to 1:25,000 scale and the ability to cache pages.

Advice for Car Drivers

Traveling by car is the easiest way to tour the Aisne battlefields. French driving regulations are subject to change, so it is best to check on the AA website, or equivalent, for the current situation.

Some general pointers include:

- Ensure that your car insurance is fully valid (this particularly applies to comprehensive insurance).
- Check what mandatory items cars have to carry, e.g. spare light bulbs; fluorescent vests carried in the car for driver and all passengers; breathalyzers; warning triangles; fire extinguishers; etc.
- Similarly, keep up to date with regulations for the transportation of animals.
- It is advisable to have your passport with you in case you are asked for identification.
- The drink drive limit is substantially less than that in the UK.
- It is absolutely prohibited to carry, transport or use radar

detectors, so Sat Nav systems should have any speed camera indicators deactivated.

- Have appropriate personal insurance and your European Health Insurance Card.

Battlefield Relics

Finally, a word of warning with regard to battlefield debris. It is unwise to handle any metallic objects in the form of bullets, shells, grenades or barbed wire found in the many woods of the Chemin des Dames. Equally, you are advised to leave alone any unexploded shells stacked up in fields or at the edge of paths awaiting collection by the French bomb disposal units. Be particularly vigilant in woodland from the end of September to the end of February, as hunting is popular and since the time of the French Revolution is considered to be a citizen's right. Be especially wary after lunch and make sure you are wearing some very visible items of clothing.

Complementary to this guide, *Aisne 1914* by Jerry Murland admirably covers the battle of 1914 and provides a thoroughly recommended walking and touring guide to the earlier, adjacent battlefield.

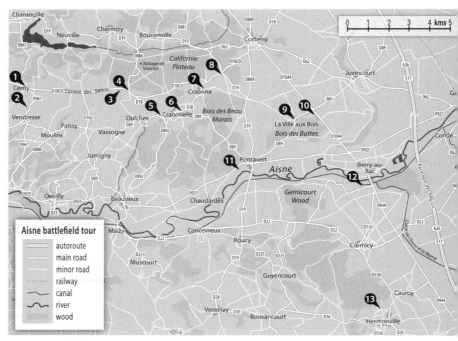

Car Tour 1: A drive round IX Corps area as on 27 May 1918

This tour covers the area occupied by the British XI Corps at the beginning of the battle on 27 May 1918. It starts at the front line positions and follows the retreat of the various divisions and brigades during the course of the day. The drive will explore the ridges of the Chemin des Dames as well as the Aisne River valley and the Aisne Canal.

Cerny-en-Laonnois – Vendresse British Cemetery – Caverne du Dragon museum – La Ferme d'Hurtebise – Basque Monument - The French National Cemetery at Craonnelle – Craonne – Chevreux - The Memorial to the 2nd Devonshire Regiment – La Musette crossroads – La Ville-aux-Bois British Cemetery – Beaurepaire French Military Cemetery – French National Tank Monument at Choléra crossroads – Berry-au-Bac French Military Cemetery – Hermonville Military Cemetery.

Depending on how long is spent at, for example, Caverne du Dragon or La Ville-aux-Bois British Cemetery, allow five to six hours.

Most British visitors arrive in the Chemin des Dames region from the north. The best exit from the A26 *Autoroute des Anglais* is junction 13, on to the N44 running south of Laon. From the N44 the route to the Chemin des Dames, via the D967, is clearly sign posted. The D967 passes through the villages of Bruyères-et-Montbérault and Chamouille before reaching the crossroads with the D18, the Chemin des Dames, at Cerny-en-Laonnois.

The Chemin des Dames rises and falls with the undulations of the ridge, but at no point is it considered hilly. The ridge varies much in breath; above Craonne it is very narrow, broadening out above Craonnelle to a width of 400 metres, and then contracting to less than 100 metres at Hurtebise Farm. On the southern slopes, alternating valleys and spurs of land drop down to the River Aisne, roughly 400 metres below.

(1.) We begin the tour at **Cerny-en-Laonnois**, which saw much fighting and was almost completely destroyed during the Great War. Next to the crossroads is a memorial chapel, with parking alongside it. On the opposite side of the main road are two cemeteries, which contain the graves of French and German soldiers spanning the whole of the war, from 1914 to 1918.

The French plot has some 5,000 burials and also fifty-four Russian graves dating from 1917. A further 2,000 soldiers are buried in a mass

Cerny German Cemetery

Cerny German
Cemetery, 1920s.

grave. The cemetery was constructed between 1919 and 1925, with substantial restoration work in 1972.

The German cemetery can be accessed through the rear of the French plot. This is one of a handful of German cemeteries in the area containing graves of combatants killed in the 1918 battle.

Johann Kappendobler, 30 May, Block 2 Grave 134.

Zur frommen Gebetserinnerung an
den ehrengeachteten Herrn

Johann Kappendobler,
Oekonomssohn von Reut,
Pfarrei Vornbach,
Obergefreiter b. bayer. Fussartillerie-
Bataillon Nr. 28, Batterie Nr. 2,

welcher am 30. Mai 1918 schwer ver-
wundet wurde und im Feldlazarett am
gleichen Tage im 37. Lebensjahre den
Heldentod fürs Vaterland starb.

Er ruhe im Frieden!

Ehre seinem Andenken!

Vergebens ist nun alles Hoffen
Auf eine frohe Wiederkehr.
Weil Dich die Kugel hat getroffen,
Ist diese Hoffnung nun nicht mehr.
Nun ruhe sanft in fremder Erde
Von diesem schweren Kampfe aus.
Uns ist nun nimmermehr beschieden
Ein freudig Wiederseh'n zu Haus.
Ruhe sanft in fremder Erde!

Zu beziehen durch J. Reitinger, Kaufmann, Vornbach.

Vendresse British Cemetery.

On leaving the cemetery take the Chemin des Dames, the D18, towards Craonne. After less than 100 metres turn left on to the D967 towards Vendresse.

(2.) Vendresse British Cemetery

Descend down the hill and after a kilometre the British cemetery comes into view on the right hand side. The views over the surrounding countryside in all directions are outstanding. This is a concentration cemetery, with the graves of 700 soldiers - 339 are unidentified - who were killed in the fighting of either 1914 or 1918. There are seventy men buried here, mostly from the Yorkshire and East Yorkshire Regiments, who were killed on 27 May 1918 or who died shortly afterwards.

Here you will find the grave of **Brigadier General Ralph Husey** (II GI), who commanded 25 Brigade on the day of the German attack. On the morning of 27 May, Husey was stationed at Brigade HQ near **Le Choléra crossroads**. Along with his Brigade Major, Captain Basil Pascoe, Husey organised a defence but during this action Pascoe was killed. Husey then rallied troops from the 8th Division in the defence of one of the key bridges over the Aisne at **Gernicourt**.

Brigadier General RH Husey, GOC 25 Brigade.

Husey was last seen firing desperately at a horde of Germans as they closed in on his position. One report suggests that, although severely wounded, he continued to resist until struck by a rifle butt to the head. He was evacuated by the Germans but died from his wounds two days later. Husey was originally buried by the Germans in the little village of Le Thour, some fifteen miles to the north-east. However, after the Armistice, his remains were exhumed and reinterred here.

Another notable casualty buried in Vendresse is **Lieutenant Colonel James Thomson** (II A2), 5/Yorks, who led a gallant defence of Craonne

Lieutenant Colonel Thomson is also remembered at Malton church.

191

village on the morning of the attack. Another Yorkshireman found here is **Captain Norman Ingleby** (I A20), 4/Yorks. He was a stalwart of Hull and East Riding Rugby Football Club.

Captain William Noel Moscrop (I D1), adjutant of 5/DLI, was reported as missing following the fighting on 27 May and later presumed killed. This was confirmed when his and other graves were found in 1919. Their location indicated that he and a number of men had died fighting in defence of the bridge at Maizy. Moscrop's body was then moved here.

Captain Richard Hewetson (IV F3) 3 Bn, attd. 9 Bn. The Loyal North Lancashire Regiment, died of wounds on 3 July 1918. His obituary in *The Times* notes:

Captain NW Ingleby, 4/Yorks.T

His division, the 25th, was sent with other tired divisions to rest on the Aisne. They were overwhelmed on May 27 by five times as many Germans. He was ordered to fill a gap which had occurred on the left flank three miles long. This was over five miles away. They had not gone more than half an hour when they met with the enemy in large forces. They put up a splendid fight which lasted nearly one hour, by which time they were practically surrounded. Captain Hewetson was taken prisoner with his leg smashed, but was not picked up until the next day, by which time gas gangrene had set in. His leg was amputated by an English doctor, also a prisoner. But, owing to lack of food, Captain Hewetson died five weeks later in a cellar converted into a field ambulance and was buried in Beaurieux Cemetery. He was 24 years of age. His colonel wrote: 'It will be a help to you in bearing the blow to be assured of the very real esteem and affection with which your son's memory will be cherished by all in the regiment who served with him. He leaves a record of steady accomplishing of good work, and his calm and reliable nature made him a most valuable officer. All my memories of him are pleasant ones.'

Captain WN Moscrop 5/DLI.

Captain R Hewetson, 9/Loyal North Lancs.

Vendresse British Cemetery in the 1920s.

Like many of the graves here, Captain Hewetson's body was later removed from Beaurieux Cemetery and moved to the peaceful surroundings of this cemetery.

(3.) Leave Vendresse Cemetery and retrace your steps back to the Chemin des Dames. After about two kilometres the **Caverne du Dragon museum** comes into view on the left hand side. This relatively new construction was built in 1999. There is little direct information here concerned with the events of May 1918. However, this is one of the few places that has toilet facilities and also a small café with a bookshop.

This museum (or rather the site of the 'Dragon's Lair' or, in German, *Drachenhöhle*), has been a tourist destination since the 1920s. During the Great War this large *creute* or subterranean quarry was occupied by both the French and the Germans and regular underground battles raged between 1915 and 1918. The area near Hurtebise Ridge was tactically important. The Chemin des Dames is relatively narrow here and it became one of the major objectives of the Nivelle Offensive in 1917.

There are regular tours of this hidden and secretive world, which last about an hour. Further details can be found on the Caverne du Dragon website: http://www.caverne-du-dragon.com

Caverne du Dragon museum.

Original Caverne du Dragon.

Continue your journey, following the Chemin des Dames. After travelling a couple of hundred metres, an impressive statue can be seen. Turn left here and park near the farm buildings.

(4.) This is **La Ferme d'Hurtebise.** During the Battle of Craonne in 1814 Napoleon stayed here overnight. The name roughly translates as *touched by the wind* and it is easy to see why, as it stands alone in an exposed position on top of one of the highest points on the Chemin des Dames ridge. Occupying such a commanding position, this area was heavily fought over throughout the war and the farm was totally obliterated, being rebuilt during the 1920s.

The majestic memorial nearby commemorates both the troops of

Marie-Louise Memorial.

Basque Monument.

Napoleon and the French *bleuets* (young private soldiers) who fought here a hundred years later. Known as the *Marie-Louise,* the statue was named after the young recruits of 1814 who had been so named in honour of the Emperor's second wife, Marie Louise. Originally a small obelisk with a star on top was unveiled near here in 1914 to honour the sacrifice of these young men but disappeared once fighting commenced here in September 1914. In 1927 a new bronze statue was erected, the work of the sculptor Maxime Real del Sarte. A soldier from the Imperial Guard and a French *poliu* - with a flag fluttering between them - reach upwards, holding a laurel crown in glorious celebration.

On the wall of the farm is a small memorial plaque placed there in honour of the Zouaves who fought bravely here in April 1917.

At this point there is a fork in the road with the D18 turning to the right and the Chemin des Dames, now the D895 on the map. You are now entering the part of the battlefield occupied by units of the British 50th Division. Follow the road as it dips to the right down the hill to the **(5.) Basque Monument.** This is a most impressive monument to the French 36th Division, made up of regiments from the south west of France. Next to the imposing obelisk, a forlorn figure dressed in traditional peasant garb gazes towards the Pyrenees, the homeland of the Basques.

This is a very good vantage point, with views over the sector of the

Tour Observatory Californie Plateau from Basque monument.

battlefield where 150 Brigade. This is near P C La Terrasse, the important position to which Brigadier General Rees was making on the morning of the attack before he was taken prisoner. This would have allowed him to observe the German forces streaming over the ridges of the Californie Plateau, which can be seen directly ahead, with the new wooden viewing platform prominent. Down below in the valley is Craonnelle and above to the right is the brooding statue of Napoleon (see Walk 1 for details).

After leaving the monument return to the D18 and follow the road as it winds through a series of bends to Craonnelle. Above the settlement the ridges of the Chemin des Dames are clearly visible. **(6.) The French National Cemetery at Craonnelle** (See Walk 1 for

French National Cemetery Craonnelle.

details) is on the left just as you leave the village. Follow the road as it bends round and up to **(7.) Craonne.** A little further on, between trees lining both sides of the road, is *Ancien Craonne*. This is now the site of an arboretum, which commemorates the ruins of this lost village, utterly destroyed during the course of the war.

It is possible to stop here and follow a walk, which takes in the main sites of the Californie Plateau where 150 Brigade were positioned on 27 May. (See Walk 1)

After a kilometre you arrive at a cross roads where the D18 and D19 meet. This is the site of the former village of **(8.) Chevreux,** which was fortified and incorporated into the defensive system of the Chemin des Dames sector. This is the eastern limit of the hilly country associated with the Chemin des Dames ridges. There is a small monument at the crossroads, which records the fact that there was once a settlement here. Craonne's railway station and a cannery are both associated with this site. This was also where 150 Brigade's sector merged with that of the 151. B Company of the 8/DLI manned this defensive position, an important part of the British Battle Zone. According to the history of the battalion: '...from which position posts were pushed forward at night to the Craonne-Corbeny road and withdrawn by day as sentry groups at the top of the hill had a full view over the entire front'.

It is now thickly wooded and it is difficult to appreciate its relative elevation on a slight hill that allowed observation over German positions in Corbeny, roughly one kilometre distant. Despite this, the history records that, during the opening phase of the battle, not a single officer from B Company escaped from the sector and that after the preliminary bombardment: 'The casualties in these trenches were appallingly heavy.'

At the crossroads turn right, following the D19 towards La Ville-aux-Bois-lès-Pontavert. This road follows the Battle Zone of 151

Memorial to the 2nd Devonshire Regiment, at La Ville aux Bois, erected in 1922.

Brigade and 149 Brigades. On the right is the Bois de Beaumarais, which hid artillery positions of the 50th Division. Not too far away is La Renaissance Ferme, which was near the boundary between 8/DLI and 6/DLI. At the next crossroads take the smaller road almost straight ahead. The two villages appearing on the horizon to the left are Corbeny and, further to the right, Juvincourt, both held by the enemy. To the left Le Temple Ferme can be observed and the second wooded area to the left is the Butte de l'Edmond. As you approach La Ville-aux-Bois-lès-Pontavert, the road becomes more rutted due to it being used by heavy farm vehicles. You are now passing through the Battle Zone of 149 Brigade; to the right were positioned the redoubts of Centre Marceau and Centre de Quimper (the redoubts in this sector were named after towns in Normandy). Both of these fortified defences were held by companies of 6/NF. To the left the middle ground was held by the forwardmost battalion of the brigade, 4/NF.

The landscape here gently undulates but behind the ridges of the Chemin des Dames now stand out prominently on the horizon. The wood ahead, just to the south of the village, is the Bois des Buttes, where units of 23 Brigade, 8th Division made a last ditch stand on 27 May. You will enter the village via the Route de Craonne; at the junction turn right into the Rue Saint-Jean. The Mairie is on your right and opposite is **(9.) The Memorial to the 2nd Devonshire Regiment** (see Walk 2 for more details). On the wall of the Mairie there is a plaque to the 5th (Gibraltar) Field Artillery Battery.

Continue in the direction you have come, following through the village on the D89 for about one kilometre until you reach a junction with the D1044, a busy highway that connects Reims with Laon. This is **La Musette Crossroads**, where the memorial to the Devons originally stood; turn right here. Almost immediately on the right is a Commonwealth War Graves Cemetery.

La Ville-aux-Bois British Cemetery. Note bunkers to the back, right.

(10.) La Ville-aux-Bois British Cemetery

This cemetery has one of the highest number of unknown in proportion to known graves amongst CWGC cemeteries of the Western Front. There are 564 Commonwealth burials of which 413 are unidentified. Most are from the 50th and 8th Divisions, with a few from the 21st Division. This is a burial ground almost exclusively containing soldiers killed in the Aisne Battle 1918 (there are also two burials from the Second War). There are also four memorials to four British soldiers believed to have been buried here, as well as other special memorials which record the names of eighteen others who were once buried in German cemeteries whose graves have been lost. A number of soldiers now resting in this cemetery died in German Prisoner of War camps and were reinterred here after the war. There are two concrete bunkers behind the cemetery wall to the rear.

Amongst those buried here are two battalion commanders: **Lieutenant Colonel Christopher Galbraith "Gary" Buckle DSO, MC** (II A10), of 2/Northamptons, was a regular soldier who joined the regiment in 1909 and was 30 years of age when he died on the morning

of 27 May 1918. He had distinguished himself at Vermelles in 1915 (MC) and was awarded the DSO for leadership of 2/Northamptons during an attack in early 1917, probably at Bouchavesnes on 4 March 1917. These encounters had led to him being wounded five times; once by a sniper and he sustained serious wounds to the ankle on 19 September 1917 from a wayward signal rocket and was laid up for a week. During April 1918 Buckle commanded the 6/Northamptons but on 3 May he was transferred back to 2/Northamptons

Lieutenant Colonel Gary Buckle's grave, discovered by his mother in 1919.

who were in the process of moving to the Aisne. On the morning of 27 May Buckle, pistol in hand, was killed outside his headquarters in a trench surrounded by dead Germans. Buckle's father, Major General C R Buckle, who commanded the Royal Artillery of the Second Army in 1918, visited the Aisne in November just after the Armistice. He managed to locate the dugout where his son had been killed and his grave marked with a small wooden cross (now kept in Warcop Church, Cumbria) and his helmet, which had two bullet holes near the crown. He also ventured into the interior of the dugout and discovered various communications from 8th Division HQ and the note pad used by his son with the final message, timed at 1.30 am, sent to his men: 'No short bombardment can possibly cut our wire and if the sentries are alert it cannot be cut by hand. If they try to, shoot the devils.'

Lieutenant Colonel CG Buckle DSO MC.

In 1919 Mrs Elizabeth Braithwaite Buckle, Gary Buckle's mother, made what was one of the earliest battlefield pilgrimages to the Western Front. She recorded her experiences in a small booklet produced in 1919, *A Kingly Grave in France*:

My son's grave was so remote from any cemetery then being concentrated, we begged that it might be left undisturbed and that we might purchase the ground. The Commission had so far only erected a better wooden cross marker than the one placed there by the Colonel's men, and registered it in their books. They agreed to my request and had no objection to my going to see it.

We had a mile to walk to the front line [near La Ville-aux-Bois] headquarters. We had had two barbed wire entanglements and several old trenches to cross. The first thing that forcibly struck me was the enormous extent of open country without a yard of cover in which men of the Eighth Division had to lay out in the open under one of the most intensive bombardments of the war, before the Germans advanced in force at dawn. I saw no graves as I made my way. I saw one cross with a German name scrawled on it, but there were helmets here and there, rusted rifles and scraps of cartridge belts all hidden among the wild flowers. Suddenly I was at the end of my quest. There, beside his trench, facing the miles of open country, lay our only son. Over the

Lieutenant Colonel BD
Gibson DSO Croix de
Guerre.

wooden cross they had slung his helmet bullet riddled as we had known it would be. A few yards away were the bodies of Germans, as though the Colonel had shot them first? My thoughts went out to their mothers or loved ones, and I wondered and wept.

Lieutenant Colonel Bertrand Gibson DSO, Croix de Guerre with Palms (I E15), Commanding Officer 4/NF is buried here too. He had fallen leading a spirited defence, first at Centre Marceau, then at Butte de l'Edmond, where he died, shot through the head. His citation for the Croix de Guerre reads:

This officer was in command of his Battalion, which was holding the front line trenches on May 27th, 1918, in the Aisne sector. He continued to send information of the enemy's advance until his Headquarters was completely surrounded. He then collected all available men of his Headquarters party and, although attacked on three sides, it was due to this officer's personal example and total disregard of danger that the enemy was delayed in their advance for a considerable time. He was shot through the head and killed whilst standing on the parapet to get a better view of the enemy, who at the time were advancing up a communication trench.

Lieutenant Colonel Bertrand Gibson.

Another officer from the 50th Division to be found here, **Major Robert Dickson** (I I7)

7/DLI, was killed whilst trying to hold off a German attack on the bridge at Maizy.

Captain Norman Constantine, MC (I K4), 4/Yorks, was the youngest of three brothers from East Harlsey near Northallerton who all served in the same battalion. He won his MC in the Somme fighting of 1916. At the time of the German attack on the Aisne he was in charge of the battalion's transport and it was in attending to this role, whilst bringing up rations from La Hutte to Craonne, that he was killed by a German shell.

Captain N Constantine MC.

Brigade Major (25 Brigade), Captain Basil Conquest Pascoe, MC, Adjutant (I C8), 2/Rifle Brigade, is buried here. His obituary, from Harrow School, states:

On 27th May, 1918, the British line was heavily attacked by the Germans and Major Pascoe left the Brigade Headquarters to rally the men and was last seen in the open trying to extend the line.

One of the Special Memorials is to **Major Hon. George Boscawen, DSO** (Notre Dame de Liesse Mem 9), commanding 116 Siege Battery, Royal Garrison Artillery at the time of his death. The History of 77 Brigade, RGA, gives the following account of the battery's actions that night:

During the night of May 26-27 the battery at Craonne fired at a slow rate until the ammunition had been expended at about 4 am. The enemy attacked between 4 am and 5 am. on the 27th, and when the barrage (which had been very heavy on the battery all night) lifted about 7.30 am the enemy was seen on the right rear of the battery position. The guns were then blown up with the rounds reserved for this purpose, and the battery retired to a bank in the rear,

Brigade Major (25 Brigade) Captain BC Pascoe MC.

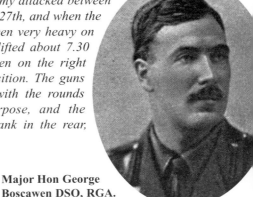

Major Hon George Boscawen DSO, RGA.

where they made a stand with rifles. Major Hon. G. Boscawen, D.S.O., was badly wounded and died later as a prisoner at Laon. 2nd Lieut. Hearn and 2nd Lieut. Gibson were killed with about eight men. (Information from those repatriated.) 2nd Lieut. Wilson and seventy men were taken prisoner. Major Hon. G E Boscawen died of his wounds as a POW at Liesse on 7 Jun 1918.

Boscawen is the family name of the Viscount Falmouth: George was the second son of the 7th Viscount.

After visiting La Ville-aux-Bois Cemetery head back along the D89 to La Ville-aux-Bois-lès-Pontavert. Continue through the village in the direction of Pontavert. It is not long before you enter a wooded area and on your left is the Bois des Buttes. The actions of the 2/Devons and 2/Middlesex here are recounted in the walks section. Once out of the wooded part of the drive

Also buried here, Driver WW Herbert, D Battery 75 Brigade RFA.

you should be able to see a white water tower and the village of Pontavert. The small wood on your left, just before you enter Pontavert, is the Butte de l'Edmond where the remnants of 149 Brigade were overrun. On the morning of the battle units from 23 Brigade and the 50th Division fell back along this road to the bridge on the Aisne at Pontavert. Sidney Rogerson, writing in *The Last of the Ebb* noted:

Accordingly, the main body moved off [from 23rd Brigade Headquarters] *with the Brigadier* [General Grogan] *leading and two of the clerks bearing the tin dispatch box. Although flying splinters of shell rang on steel helmets and clipped great pieces from the road, the little gas-goggled procession wound its way to Pontavert untouched.*

At the junction with the D925 turn left and follow the road, signposted Beaurieux, for about two kilometres.

(11.) Beaurepaire French Military Cemetery, Pontavert is on the southern side of the D925 after leaving the village. This cemetery dates from 1915 and was enlarged after the war. It contains the graves of 7,000 French soldiers. There is a small Commonwealth War Graves Plot at the east corner of the cemetery. Most of its sixty five graves date from May and June 1918, with some thirty-five unidentified. There was a PoW work camp nearby at Pontavert and a number of the graves are of these prisoners. There are two Special Memorials erected to two PoWs formerly buried at Guyencourt French Military Cemetery, whose

Beaurepaire French Cemetery, Pontavert.

Ruet Jeune, phot.

graves could not be found: Private J McDougal of 15/DLI, and Private T Jones of 9 Royal Welch Fusiliers.

Return to the D925 and head back to Pontavert. Continue through the village, following the main road in the direction of Berry-au-Bac. On your right is the flood

**Private T Jones
9/Welch Fus.**

Beaurepaire cemetery with British graves.

The destroyed village of Gernicourt, viewed from the canal.

plain of the Aisne. Notice the higher ground in this direction. The German Army was across these ridges by nightfall on the first day of the battle. After a few minutes you come close to Gernicourt Wood, where units of 22/DLI, 2/East Lancs Regiment and 15 Field Company RE attempted to stem the German advance. A fierce battle raged amongst the trenches, deep dugouts and shattered woodland. Eventually the British forces were overwhelmed by German stormtroopers who had managed to cross the Aisne at Pontavert and attacked the defenders from the rear.

After five kilometres the **French National Tank Monument at Choléra crossroads** is reached. The memorial commemorates the first use of tanks by the French Army in April 1917, as part of the Nivelle Offensive. A little further along this road, to the east, is where 25 Brigade HQ was located. Notice the slightly undulating nature of the

Trench map of Gernicourt Wood and Berry-au-Bac

Berry-au-Bac French Military Cemetery during construction.

ground in this area, ideal terrain for tank warfare. The Germans also used tanks here during the first day of the Aisne, mustered in the village of Juvincourt to the north east.

At the crossroads take the right turn, the D1044 in the direction of **Berry-au-Bac**. Within two kilometres the centre of the village is reached. Berry-au-Bac was a busy settlement in 1914, sited at the confluence of the Canal Lateral and the Canal de l'Aisne à la Marne and where two railways, to Laon, Soissons and Reims, met. By the end of 1914 the village lay in ruins. After the war Berry-au-Bac lay in the so called *Zone Rouge* but, despite this, the village was rebuilt between 1921 and 1930.

Continue through the village until you reach a small bridge over the Aisne. Take an immediate right on the southern side of the bridge, direction Gernicourt, on the D1140. After a few hundred metres you arrive at **(12.) Berry-au-Bac French Military Cemetery**.

This cemetery was started during the war and was originally known as Cimetière Militaire de Moscou, after a nearby hamlet. It was designated a National Cemetery in 1925. It contains the graves of 3,933 French soldiers, of whom some 1,958 are unidentified and lie in two ossuaries. The British graves are located in the north west part. All of the men in this plot were killed in the Aisne fighting of 1918, between 27 and 29 May, of whom seventeen are unknown.

This cemetery is not far from the front line held by British troops on the first day of the battle, a few kilometres due east of here. This is where the 8th Division, to the north, met the 21st Division stationed to the south of Berry-au-Bac. This area, around Cote 108 and Sapigneul,

Berry-au-Bac cemetery today.

British graves.

had been heavily fought over since 1915 and the remains of a number of large craters from mines detonated by both the French and the Germans are clearly visible and were a feature of the fighting in this sector. The British 62 Brigade held the front here, with the 12/13 Northumberland Fusiliers occupying the ground around Cote 108. The total number of casualties for this unit in three days of action was

Mine crater at Cote 108. The area is now heavily wooded and in private hands.

Open country near Cormicy. The small hill of Mont Espin in the distance.

eighteen officers and 493 OR. Nine of the graves in this cemetery are of men from north east England, with one casualty from the 2/Rifle Brigade and two officers of the Royal Air Force.

It would appear that **Second Lieutenant Christopher Beaumont (23/24)** and his Observer, **Second Lieutenant Frank Whitehouse (23/24)**, were flying a RE 8 B5147 (Reconnaissance Experimental) from Fismes aerodrome where 52 Squadron RAF were based on a patrol over the Chemin des Dames on the morning of 27 May when they were shot down over Craonne.

After visiting the cemetery, return to the main road through Berry-au-Bac and head south along the D944 in the direction of Reims. You are now running parallel with the positions occupied by the 21st Division. The landscape here is flat, almost barren. You are now entering the Marne Department and Reims is seventeen kilometres distant. Just to the east is the Aisne-Marne canal, which wanders through this low ground. 62, 110 and 64 brigades all had units stationed across the canal here, in many respects a very precarious position. The British trenches were overlooked by German positions occupying the higher ground on Mount Spin (Espin on modern maps) and further to the south at Fort Brimont. As you head south down the Reims road, on your right hand side can be seen another large French National Cemetery, **Cimetière National de la Maison Bleue.** The rising ground to the left was the German held strong point of Mont Spin. Just before the cemetery, the D32 heads towards **Cormicy**, which can be seen two kilometres distant. This village was defended by the Leicestershire battalions of 110 Brigade. Continue on the main road until you meet the turning for the D530, to your right, with directions for **Cauroy-lès-Hermonville.** This village formed part of the Battle Zone held by 64 Brigade. A staunch defence was organised here by 15/DLI, with support from companies of the pioneer battalion, 14/NF, and was only given up in the early evening of 27 May.

(13.) Hermonville Military Cemetery is located in the northern part of the village, overlooked by a number of vineyards on a

neighbouring hillside. A peaceful and idyllic setting, the Commonwealth War Graves Commission provides good directions to this cemetery:

Enter Hermonville along the Rue de Reims and at the village centre turn right (first CWGC direction sign) going along the Rue de L'Eglise on the D530, which leads onto the Rue de Sébastopol; and then the Rue St Remy. At the following junction turn right into Rue Charles de Gaulle and 20 metres further on turn left up the Rue des Dourdonnes. The cemetery is at the end of this 150 metre long narrow road.

The cemetery originally also contained 407 French and ninety-nine German graves but these have been removed. There are 250 war casualties commemorated here, 138 of whom are unidentified. There are Special Memorials erected to five soldiers from the Royal Engineers, all killed on 27 May 1918, but whose graves can no longer be found, and also to six soldiers from the United Kingdom who are believed to be buried amongst the unknown graves.

Hermonville Military Cemetery, with vineyards in the background.

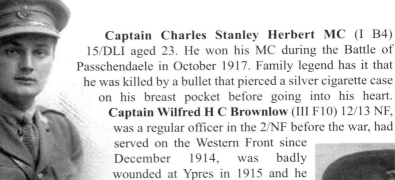

Captain Charles Stanley Herbert MC (I B4) 15/DLI aged 23. He won his MC during the Battle of Passchendaele in October 1917. Family legend has it that he was killed by a bullet that pierced a silver cigarette case on his breast pocket before going into his heart.

Captain Wilfred H C Brownlow (III F10) 12/13 NF, was a regular officer in the 2/NF before the war, had served on the Western Front since December 1914, was badly wounded at Ypres in 1915 and he only returned to the front on 15 May 1918. He was killed organizing a rearguard action on 28 May at the Massif de St Thierry. A brother officer reported that, 'He was hit by a piece of shell and knew at once he was dying and said, "Give my people my love and tell them I died with a smile on my face".'

Captain CS Herbert MC, 15/DLI.

Captain WHC Brownlow 12/13 North Fusiliers.

Private Percy Ryland (II D6), 15/DLI, was one of the youngest soldiers to die on 27 May, he had just turned eighteen. Also of the 15/DLI was **Sergeant Andrew Robson MM** (II D2) from Coldstream killed 27 May.

Second Lieutenant John Arthur Pighills (III G8) (attach. 11/Lancs Fusiliers) died of wounds in German captivity on 29 May. **Private Watson Towers** (III B9), 1/Worcesters, was killed in the opening moments of the attack on 27 May.

Also buried here is **Private Frank O'Neill** (III G6), of the 1/Sherwood Foresters, who was shot at dawn on the 16th May 1918 at Hermonville. There were two convictions recorded against O'Neill for violence and desertion. He had disappeared when his battalion were digging trenches and was arrested four days later in civilian clothes. He was unrepresented at his trial on 26 April 1918 and was the last man to be executed from the 8th Division.

This completes the car tour of the Aisne battlefield.

Private Percy Ryland, 15/DLI.

Sergeant Andrew Robson MM, 15/DLI.

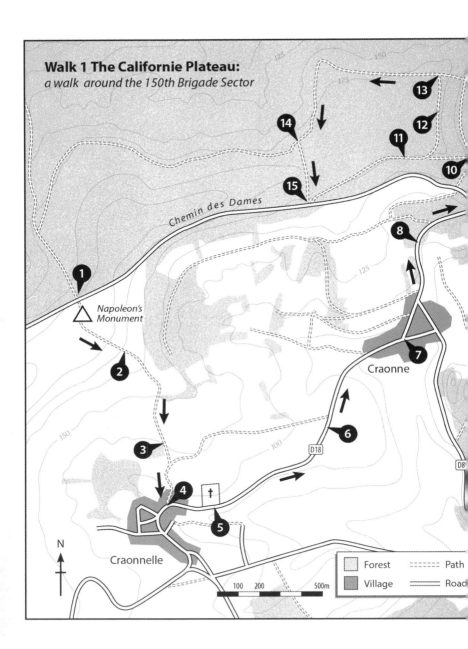

Walk 1 The Californie Plateau:
a walk around the 150th Brigade Sector

Chemin des Dames

Napoleon's Monument

Craonne

D18

D8

Craonnelle

N

| | Forest | ------- Path |
| | Village | ====== Road |

100 200 500m

212

Walk 1 The Californie Plateau:
a walk around the 150 Brigade Sector

This walk commences at Napoleon's statue on the Chemin des Dames. It is a circular walk and will take about three hours

(1.) There is a small parking place available across the D18, the **Chemin des Dames**, on the opposite side of the road to the monument of Napoleon. This statue was erected in 1974 and was the work of the sculptor Georges Thurotte. It was built on the site of the Vauclair windmill, and was used as an observation post by the French Emperor during the Battle of Craonne, which was fought here on 7 March 1814. French arms were successful in this clash against the Prussian and Russian forces led by Field Marshal Blücher. It proved to be a pyrrhic victory and was the last battle won by Napoleon before his exile to Elba.

On the morning of 27 May 1918, the ground immediately on the south side of the Chemin des Dames was occupied by 1/4 East Yorks on the morning of 27 May 1918. Trench Falaise runs parallel with the D18 for 200 metres, and the reserve companies of the East Yorkshires were sheltering here in deep dugouts cut into the side of the trench wall. The area to your right, as you face the statue, was occupied by units of the French 22nd Division.

(2.) Follow the track to the right of the monument. Just before the path begins to descend, after 150 metres, it is possible to make sense of the sector occupied by the 150th Brigade. Here the landscape opens up behind you, and an extensive panorama can be seen. To the right the new **Tour Observatoire**, on the crest of **Californie Plateau**, juts prominently out of the woodland, some 1 kilometre distant. To your left, about the same distance away, the monument to the Basque regiments who served here can also be observed. The area between these

George Thurotte's Napoleon monument, with the Chemin des Dames in background.

View of the Basque Monument and the Chemin des Dames.

two landmarks roughly corresponds to the sector held by troops of 150 Brigade.

(3.) As you follow the track as it drops in height, you are now heading due south. On your right a number of vineyards associated with **Craonnelle** can be seen, and the village itself comes into view. This is a gentle slope, but it allows you to appreciate the depth of the battlefield and provides good views in all directions. The British troops were forced off the ridge north of the Chemin des Dames and came tumbling down these slopes, often intermingling with French units who had also been ousted from their positions by advancing German stormtoopers. German cavalry also played a role here, later in the morning.

(4.) The farm track you have been following eventually peters out after another 300 metres, becoming a pavéd road, **Rue de L'Ecole**. Follow this road round to a junction and turn left on to the main road

Craonnelle village with its ruined church.

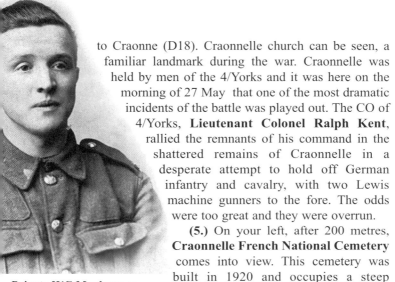

to Craonne (D18). Craonnelle church can be seen, a familiar landmark during the war. Craonnelle was held by men of the 4/Yorks and it was here on the morning of 27 May that one of the most dramatic incidents of the battle was played out. The CO of 4/Yorks, **Lieutenant Colonel Ralph Kent**, rallied the remnants of his command in the shattered remains of Craonnelle in a desperate attempt to hold off German infantry and cavalry, with two Lewis machine gunners to the fore. The odds were too great and they were overrun.

(5.) On your left, after 200 metres, **Craonnelle French National Cemetery** comes into view. This cemetery was built in 1920 and occupies a steep hillside above the village. The cemetery was sited next to a First Aid Post that was used during the Nivelle Offensive of April 1917. Men buried here came from battles fought to the north, on the Chemin des Dames ridges; particularly the Plateau de Casemates and Californie Plateau. In the early 1920s other soldiers' remains were gathered here from smaller cemeteries nearby, such as Craonne, Oulches and Vassogne.

Private WC Maybray, a signaller with 4/Yorks.

Craonnelle French National Cemetery. Note the steepness of the gradient.

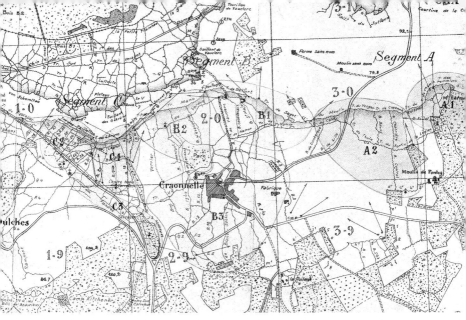

French trench map c.1916. Note the cemetery to the east of Craonnelle

It contains the graves of 3,811 French soldiers (of whom 1,809 are unidentified). There are twenty-four British burials, seventeen of whom are unidentified; the seven whose names are known died on 27 May 1918. The British graves are scattered amongst the French dead in different parts of the cemetery. Four men came from 1/4 East Yorks, who held the British forward positions on the plateau to the north on the morning of the German attack.

Private 29568 Robert Watson (1844) of the 1/4 East Yorks, was employed by the North Eastern Railway and hailed from Newcastle upon Tyne. From the records held by the CWGC, it appears that Robert Watson had been previously buried a kilometre north west of Craonne until his body was then reburied in the French cemetery at Craonnelle. According to the Graves Registration Report, this grave was only officially recorded at Craonnelle French National Cemetery on 6 May 1925.

One of the other men buried here is **Private 67830 Charles Gordon Sills** (1720) of 50th Battalion Machine Gun Corps. An interesting letter contained in his service record states that his grave was found in a 'lonely place' and that

216

Private R Watson,
1/4 East Yorks.

the cross marking his place of burial was made by the Germans. The letter appears to have been written in either 1919 or the early 1920s by Lady Alice Douglas-Pennant, who was visiting the place where her relative, Major Hon. George Edward Boscawen, was killed. (Major Boscawen RFA, died on 6th June 1918, and is buried in La Ville-aux-Bois British Cemetery.) Lady Alice Douglas-Pennant describes the area just after the war:

Craonnelle wood lies on a beautiful slope and has a wonderful view, but the wood is shattered by the terrific bombardment before the German attack. I went there because one of my relations was mortally wounded that day.

Private Charles G Sills, 50th MGC.

Eton College War Memorial records:

HON. GEORGE EDWARD BOSCAWEN/ MAJOR. D.S.O. ROYAL FIELD ARTILLERY/ BORN 6TH DEC. 1888. MORTALLY WOUNDED/ AT CRAONELLE NEAR LAON. 31ST MAY 1918.

On leaving the cemetery turn left and follow the road to Craonne. This is the longest part of the walk on the road without any paths. The traffic here is intermittent and mainly agricultural in nature. Views to the left are superb, showing the dramatic rise of the Chemin des Dames Ridge, which fills the horizon. To the right the landscape is gently rolling fields and woods.

(6.) One of the best places to pause here is by a wayside shrine. This

German reserve troops marching through Craonnelle, 27 May.

area was held by two companies of 4/Yorks in the early hours of 27 May, before they were forced back to Craonnelle. This was a secondary line of defence, the Mount Hermel-Trench Déhard Line. This trench system straddled the main Craonne road and runs to the north of Craonnelle, on your right hand side, and to the left hand side, just inside the wood, which is some 300 metres distant. This is the Bois de Beaumarais and the strongpoint of Mount Hermel is to be located just inside it. Another 500 metres due south, today concealed by the wood, was 150 Brigade HQ, La Hutte. In the early morning of 27 May 1918, Brigadier General HC Rees attempted to move from this position to what he hoped would provide him with a better view of the fighting at P C La Terrasse. This observation post can just about be picked out, lying to the south of the Basque Memorial.

(7.) Continue up the road until you arrive at the 'new' village of **Craonne**. This is a small habitation with a population of just under a hundred. It was constructed between 1921 and 1927 in a location about 400 metres south of the original village, which was deemed too dangerous to rebuild. This was part of the 'Red Zone', land that was seen as being impossible to farm or develop after the ravages of the war. On your left, in the centre of the village, is the Mairie, which contains an interesting 'maquette' or diorama of the battlefield. This shows the main trenches, bunkers and machine gun emplacements on the edge of the Californie Plateau. Tunnels to large underground caverns or *creutes* can be observed, which were a common feature of the Chemin des Dames battlefield and much utilized by troops of both sides.

(8.) **Vieux or old Craonne** is about 400 metres further north. Old

Trenches and shell holes in the arboretum at old Craonne.

Craonne is owned by the French National Forestry Office and has been turned into an arboretum. There is a walk outlined with maps and supporting panels which display photographs of the old village. This is not an integral part of the walk and can be by-passed by following the main road to the north of the village. Old Craonne was held by 5/Yorks on the opening day of the battle, as was the eastern extremity of Californie Plateau. The CO, Lieutenant Colonel J Thomson, desperately tried to contain the onward rush of German troops from his battalion headquarters in a dugout in Craonne but shortly after 5.45am most of the 5/Yorks in the defences of the village were overwhelmed.

(9.) At the crossroads on the edge of the arboretum, turn left across the D18, keeping an eye out for oncoming traffic, and follow the road to the car park, which has a number of information panels concerned with the Chemin des Dames and Californie Plateau. Much of the information here and elsewhere on the plateau is concerned with the events of the Nivelle Offensive of 1917.

(10.) Follow the footpath by the side of the panels, on the right of the car park, to the **Californie Plateau**. After about a hundred metres take a small footpath on your left through the woods. This is a fairly steep climb upwards and on wet days sturdy footwear is essential. As you reach the crest of the hill (about 150 metres) you will pass a German concrete bunker, which was originally a machine gun post. The commemorative plaque informs the reader that this emplacement was captured by the French 18th Infantry Regiment in May 1917.

(11.) Standing prominently in the front of you is the new wooden **La Tour Observatoire,** built in the spring of 2013. Again there are a number of information panels nearby and from these and the observatory magnificent views can be obtained. This is a heavily wooded area, so for a clearer view a visit in the early spring or winter is advised. It is possible to see Pontavert and the Aisne River due south; to the right, Napoleon's statue and the monument to the Basques are also visible. The rising ground on the horizon forms the heights above the town of Roucy, where the 8th Division had their HQ in Roucy Chateau. To the left the ground is more even, almost flat; this is the area of the battlefield occupied by 151 and 149 Brigades of the 50th Division, as well as units of the 8th and 21st Divisions.

You are now standing on Californie Plateau, sometimes referred to as the Craonne Plateau. The name derives from Henri Vasnier, the rich patron of the Pommery Champagne House during the late 19th century. He brought back from America a number of plants and trees that were grown on a plantation on the east side of Craonne; hence the name California Garden and later Californie Plateau.

The new Observation tower, Californie Plateau.

To the Germans the Californie Plateau was called the Winterberg. One explanation for this is that the first German troops who occupied this chalky upland were from the Sauerland (about 110 kilometres north east of Cologne), a hilly region associated with skiing and where the town of Winterberg was the major winter sport resort. It is difficult to imagine what this area was like in the late spring of 1918. Now all the slopes are densely forested, but then after three years of continuous bombardment the vegetation had been totally stripped away, leaving an indented white, chalky dome. The best description of this higher ground above the Aisne comes from Major General AD von Unruh, Chief of IV Reserve Corps (Corps von Conta) quoted in Sidney Rogerson's *The Last of the Ebb*:

Vestiges of war on the Californie Plateau, early 1920s.

Cemetery on Californie Plateau, now relocated to Craonnelle.

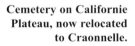

At first sight the heights of the Chemin des Dames and the Winterberg seemed to be dead. There were no signs of life. I saw only the white chalk crest of the Winterberg, so dazzling in the sunshine that it looked as if covered in snow – a fact which had probably given the name to the hill on and around which so much blood had flowed in the preceding years of war. It seemed to tower over the whole district and with its steep slopes, close-pitted with a hundred-thousand holes of bomb, grenade, and shell, and barred by formidable wire-entanglements, looked to be impregnable.

(12.) Facing away from the observatory, looking inwards, find the pathway in the right hand corner of the cleared woodland. This path will take you into the interior of the plateau. It is a relatively easy walk with few gradients. On the left hand side as you progress it is easy to pick out a number of trenches by the path in the undergrowth of the

221

wood. Two forward companies of 5/Yorks occupied this area and were the first units of IX Corps to be overpowered by German troops who had scrambled up the sides of the plateau from the north and east. Many men still lay in deep dugouts sheltering from the great avalanche of enemy shells that preceded this attack.

(13.) When you come to a wooden marker facing you (about 300 metres from the observatory) take the left hand track as directed. At the Y junction fifty metres further on, take the right hand path, where more remains of trenches can be seen on your right. Continue on this path as it loops to the left, you are now following the forward positions occupied by men from 1/4 East Yorks and 5/Yorks. Again remnants of trenches and strongpoints can be seen in the woods on either side of the path. After about 500 metres there is a junction, and on your right you will see an information board. This is concerned with the Plateau de Californie and the events of October 1917, when the French wrested the heights of the Chemin des Dames from the Germans.

(14.) Follow the signs for *Retour Parking*, which is straight ahead. This path is now much wider than the trails followed in the woods. After about 150 metres you will come to a modern sculpture by Haim Kern, which pays homage to the combatants of the Chemin des Dames battles. This was inaugurated on 5 November 1998 to commemorate

Information boards and plan of footpaths.

The Californie Plateau is still a warren of underground caverns and tunnels.

Detail of sculpture by Haim Kern, next to the viewpoint on the Chemin des Dames.

the 80th anniversary of the end of the First World War. However, at the time of going to print, this monument was stolen on 12 August 2014 and melted down for bronze.

(15.) Just after the sculpture you will emerge at the Californie Plateau car park. Follow the stairs down to the viewpoint on the other side of the D18 road. On a clear day there are superb views across the Aisne valley from here. There is also an orientation table, which details the main towns and villages that can be seen in the distance.

From here there are two

Information boards, mainly concerned with the Nivelle Offensive of 1917 and viewpoint looking south to the Aisne.

options for your return to Napoleon's statue and your vehicle. You can either follow the D18 to the left of the orientation table or retrace your steps through the woods to the Plateau de Californie information table and turn left down the path which follows a circuitous route, and after about 600 metres you will return to your transport. Again vestiges of trenches and entrances to underground dugouts can be seen.

If you decide to follow the Chemin des Dames (D18), stick to the

French trench map of Californie Plateau, January 1918

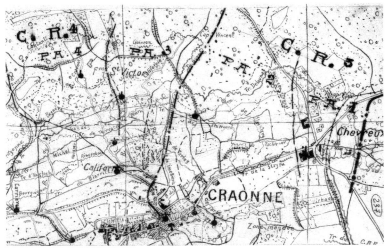

roadside verge as this can be a relatively busy road, especially during holiday periods. On the left hand side of the road the remains of the trenches can be seen. The support companies of the 1/4 East Yorks occupied these positions, the main line of resistance being Trench Falasie. After 500 metres the statue of Napoleon comes back into view.

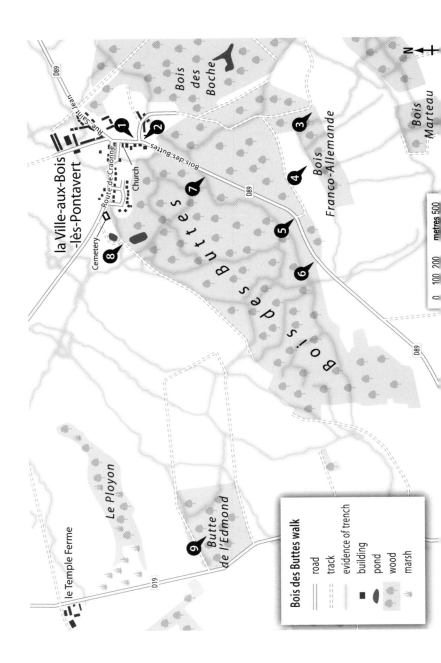

la Ville-aux-Bois-lès-Pontavert

Bois des Boche

Bois Marteau

Bois Franco-Allemande

Bois des Buttes

Bois des Buttes

Le Ployon

le Temple Ferme

Butte de l'Edmond

Church

Cemetery

Route de Craonne

Rue Saint-Jean

D89

D89

D89

D19

N

Bois des Buttes walk

- road
- track
- evidence of trench
- building
- pond
- wood
- marsh

0   100 200 metres 500

Walk 2 The Bois des Buttes

This walk commences at the Mairie in La Ville-aux-Bois-lès-Pontavert and follows a fairly circuitous route round part of the Bois des Buttes for roughly 5 kilometres. You should plan to spend about three hours here.

Opposite the Mairie in La Ville-aux-Bois-lès-Pontavert is the **2nd Devonshire Regiment Memorial (1.).** This memorial originally stood at Musette crossroads near La Ville-aux-Bois Military Cemetery, but with the increasing volume of traffic on the main Laon to Reims highway the memorial was moved to its current position in 1977. A newspaper report from the time of the unveiling in November 1921 states:

The massive stone cross standing about 300 yards in front of the Bois des Buttes is composed entirely of rough hewn granite quarried in the heart of Dartmoor. On two side steps rests a massive base in one solid block of granite, weighing five tons. Rising from the base is a well-proportioned tapering cross, reaching to a total height of 17 feet.

The base is panelled on four sides. On the panel facing the roadway is inscribed General Henri Mathias Berthelot's Order of the Day, and on the reverse is the English translation, as follows:

2nd Devonshire Regiment Memorial, near La Musette crossroads.

227

2ND BATTALION DEVONSHIRE REGIMENT
ON THE 27TH MAY 1918 AT A TIME WHEN
THE BRITISH TRENCHES WERE BEING SUBJECTED
TO FIERCE ATTACKS, THE 2ND BTN. DEVONSHIRE REGIMENT
REPELLED SUCCESSIVE ENEMY ASSAULTS WITH GALLANTRY
AND DETERMINATION AND MAINTAINED AN UNBROKEN
FRONT TILL A LATE HOUR. THE STAUNCHNESS OF THIS
BATTALION PERMITTED DEFENCES SOUTH OF THE
AISNE TO BE REORGANISED AND THEIR OCCUPATION BY
REINFORCEMENTS TO BE COMPLETED.
INSPIRED BY THE SANGFROID OF THEIR GALLANT COMMANDER
LT. COL. R. H. ANDERSON - MORSHEAD D.S.O., IN THE FACE OF
AN INTENSE BOMBARDMENT, THE FEW SURVIVORS OF THE
BATTALION, THOUGH ISOLATED AND WITHOUT HOPE OF ASSISTANCE,
HELD ON TO THEIR TRENCHES NORTH OF THE RIVER AND FOUGHT
TO THE LAST WITH AN UNHESITATING OBEDIENCE TO ORDERS.
THUS THE WHOLE BATTALION, COLONEL, 28 OFFICERS AND 552 NON-
COMMISSIONED OFFICERS AND MEN, RESPONDED WITH ONE
ACCORD AND OFFERED THEIR LIVES IN UNGRUDGING SACRIFICE
TO THE SACRED CAUSE OF THE ALLIES.

On the remaining panels of the base are carved the regimental crest and the legend: 'This memorial was erected by the 2nd Battalion Devonshire Regiment in memory of the action of May 27, 1918.'

There is a representation of the Croix de Guerre avec Palme with the inscription:

General Bertlelot arriving with Earl Fortescue and officers of the Devons at the Bois des Buttes, November 1921.

La Croix de Guerre avec Palme, a été accordee par la République française au Deuxieme Bataillon du Regiment du Devonshire, pour ce fait d'armes a Tournai, le 5 Decembre, 1918.

After the memorial's unveiling ceremony.

Lieutenant UB Burke MC, describing the battle to the visitors.

The unveiling ceremony can be viewed here:

http://www.britishpathe.com/video/glorious-devons

On the wall of the Mairie a plaque commemorates 5 (Gibraltar) Battery of XLV Brigade, RFA. In both French and English, the inscription reads:

In memory of the members of the battery who gave their lives at La Ville aux Bois les Pontavert on 27th May 1918. During the offensive of May 1918 the battery was attacked by an overwhelming force. The guns continued to fire and resistance did not cease until every man was killed or captured. For this action the battery was awarded the Croix de Guerre.

The actions of both 2/Devons and 5 Battery are described in Chapter 3.

La Ville-aux-Bois-lès-Pontavert and the neighbouring woodland, the **Bois des Buttes**, were held by units of 23 Brigade on the morning of 27 May. 2/Middlesex occupied the battle zone in front of La Ville-aux-Bois, supporting 2/West Yorks, who held the front line. 2/Devons, in reserve, were based in the Bois des Buttes. It is the area of the battle zone and the deep dugouts and bunkers of the Bois des Buttes that will be explored in this walk.

Memorial on the wall of the Mairie to 5 (Gibraltar) Battery, 45 Brigade RFA.

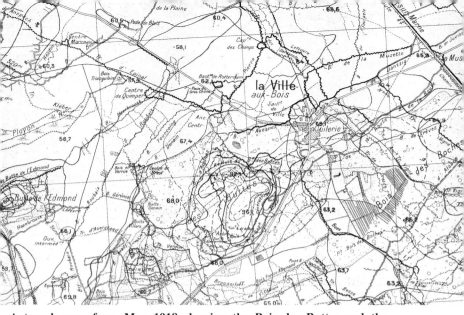

A trench map from May 1918 showing the Bois des Buttes and the surrounding area.

All of the Bois des Buttes is in private hands and therefore it is important that you follow the paths recommended here. The woodland area is unstable and not all the ordnance from the Great War has been cleared away. It is recommended that you keep extra vigilant when near the perimeter of the woods, as it is still used for hunting. Nevertheless, from the edge of the wood the detritus of battle can be observed in some of the cleared areas. Entrances to deep tunnels and bunkers are visible.

Leave the Mairie via the main road to Pontavert, the D89 and take the first turning on your left, the **Rue Chantraine (2.)**. After 200 metres the road becomes a track and heads into the woods. This is the **Bois des Boche** and was held by the reserve company of 2/Middlesex. During the morning of the attack, the wood was shrouded in smoke and gas and visibility was little more than a few yards. Follow the track for a further 500 metres until a clearing is reached. **(3.)**

The wood on your right was known as the **Bois Franco-Allemande** during the war. On your right, just before the open field, is a bunker covered in moss and bracken. This open ground which offers views back to Pontavert and the Aisne, was where **XLV Brigade RFA** was positioned on the morning of 27 May. There were three batteries of six 18-pound guns and one Howitzer battery, also of six guns. The forwardmost of these was **5 (Gibraltar) Battery** under the command of Captain John Hamon Massey. In fact this battery had five guns on

231

A German bunker near Bois Franco-Allemand.

the day of battle as one was in workshops undergoing repair. The gun-pits here were well protected, with a sandbag parapet built to the front and sides and local defence trenches had been dug. This was the scene of vicious hand to hand combat by men of the battery. As the Brigade War Diary makes clear:

> *Battery continued to fire until the position was overrun between 6.30 and 7am. Fighting with M.G. and rifles was then resorted to, and position was abandoned, when almost surrounded, by the four gunner survivors.*

Today the ground is a heavily ploughed field and there are few, if any, visible remnants of battle. Nevertheless, the line of retreat back to the Aisne, on the horizon, through the clearing can be seen. The ground here is gently rolling country with little opportunity for cover. The woods on either side of this position would have been blasted away and the woodland today is far more extensive. Some men managed to get

Looking towards the Bois des Boches from the Bois Franco Allemand. Many of the guns of XLV Brigade were positioned in this area.

The last stand of the 2nd Devons at the Bois des Buttes by **WB Wollen (1922).**

away towards the river, as Captain Hugh MacIlwaine of 2/Middlesex recalls:

> *By belly-crawling in short grass for some 300 yards, and bolting from shell-hole to shell-hole, a few of us managed to make our way to the outskirts of Pontavert, most of my men having been wiped out by the most deadly machine gun and rifle fire.*

Return to the track and follow this back about 200 metres then turn left and follow another track back towards the main La Ville-aux-Bois to Pontavert road. This track runs parallel with the Bois Franco-Allemande and the individual guns of the 5 (Gibraltar) Battery were stationed here **(4.)**. Turn left on to the main road **(5.)** It is traditionally believed that **Lieutenant Colonel Rupert Anderson-Morshead** deployed the remaining 2/Devons here in a last ditch attempt to prevent German infantry and artillery from advancing along the road to Pontavert and the Aisne. The 2/Devons swept down from the higher ground within the interior of the Bois des Buttes, having negotiated their way through the deep tunnels and dugouts of the wood. During this defensive action Anderson-Morshead was struck by machine gun fire and killed.

After 150 metres along the road to Pontavert a concrete structure on the opposite side of the road comes into view. It is widely believed that this bunker complex was the **Headquarters of 23 Brigade (6.)**. The road leaves the cover of the Bois des Buttes at this point. The woods extending to the south (on the right hand side) are a relatively recent

German bunker used by 23 Brigade HQ.

plantation. From here it is possible to see Pontavert, which is 3 kilometres distant, and the wooded uplands above the Aisne

Sidney Rogerson gives a memorable description of his hasty retreat from 23 Brigade Headquarters towards the Aisne:

View towards Pontavert. The remnants of 23 Brigade fought a running retreat from the Bois des Buttes to the Aisne.

Water filled crater in the Bois des Buttes.

What a flight that was – across shell-holes, through barbed-wire, brambles, and the twisted and shattered remains of shelters and gun-pits; stumbling, falling, sweating, the steel helmet bobbing on my head, the heavy pack between my shoulders; breathless, gasping wide-open-mouthed into the gas-mask whose clip so firmly closed my nostrils. How we got there I shall never know, but somehow there stretched before us the reeds and willows of the river, along which a steady barrage of large-calibre shells was falling, sending up tall geysers of black mud.

Return to La Ville-aux-Bois by following the D89; the village is just

Entrance to one of the many tunnels in the wood.

235

A number of German built bunkers can be observed from the road.

over one kilometre away. On both sides of the road it is possible to discern the remnants of trenches and other traces of conflict through the cover of woodland. Just to reiterate: the Bois des Buttes is privately held land and permission must be sought before entering. Enquires in this respect could be tried at the Mairie in La Ville-aux-Bois.

(**7.**) After 400 metres a signpost directs you to a grey granite memorial or *stele* on the left, just set back from the roadside verge. In these woods the French poet **Guillaume Apollinaire** was severely wounded in 1916. A local writer, Yves Gibeau, organized the erection of the memorial in 1990, which bears some famous lines of verse written by the poet.

Not long after passing the Apollinaire memorial you are once again in La Ville-aux-Bois. Continue past the 2/Devons memorial and take the second street on your left, the **Rue de Craonne**. After 150 metres you will see the village cemetery. Follow a footpath on the left, after the cemetery, towards the wood. This path skirts the perimeter of the Bois des Buttes. (**8.**) To the right, across the fields, about 750 metres away can be seen a wood, which is the **Butte de L'Edmond**. Here on the morning of 27 May, **Lieutenant Colonel Bertrand Gibson** and the remaining officers and men from 4/NF and 6/NF tried desperately to stem the flow of advancing German stormtroopers. Another, more elongated, wood can be seen to the right; this was a marshy area known as Le Ployon and nearby is **Temple Farm**.

Apart from one or two coppices, the country here is open and gently rolling. The enemy would have poured over the plain from the north.

236

EN CE LIEUDIT
LE BOIS DES BUTTES
LE 17 MARS 1916 FUT BLESSÉ
GUILLAUME
APOLLINAIRE
1880 - 1918

DIS L'AS-TU VU GUI AU GALOP
DU TEMPS QU'IL ÉTAIT MILITAIRE
DIS L'AS-TU VU GUI AU GALOP
DU TEMPS QU'IL ÉTAIT ARTIFLOT
A LA GUERRE

The memorial to the French poet Apollinaire.

The road that leaves La Ville-aux-Bois in the direction of the Chemin des Dames follows the line of redoubts that formed the British second line of resistance. Near to the village along this road was the boundary between 149 Brigade of the 50th Division and 23 Brigade of the 8th Division. Standing on the horizon, just beyond the bustling main road from Laon to Reims is **Juvincourt**, held by the Germans. At least two captured British tanks accompanied German attacking units from this village on the morning of the offensive. This was in many respects

237

For most of the war La Ville-aux-Bois had been occupied by German soldiers.

An abandoned dug out on the edge of La Ville-aux-Bois. The two small hills in the distance were in the Bois des Buttes.

The German front line ran in front of Corbeny, which can be seen in the distance.

ideal terrain for tank warfare. The remains of French tanks from the attack of April 1917 still littered the Aisne battlefield of 1918.

It is possible to walk to, and around, the Butte de L'Edmond **(9.),** but this would add another 45 minutes or more to the journey. Another additional walk would be from the centre of La Ville-aux-Bois to **La Ville-aux-Bois British Cemetery (10.),** near to the La Musette café. This is next to a busy junction of the D1044 and D89, so care must be taken, but it has the additional benefit of being one of the few places in the area to provide toilet facilities. Details of the men found buried in this cemetery are included in **Car Tour 1**. This extension would add another hour to your overall time on this walk.

View of the Chemin des Dames.

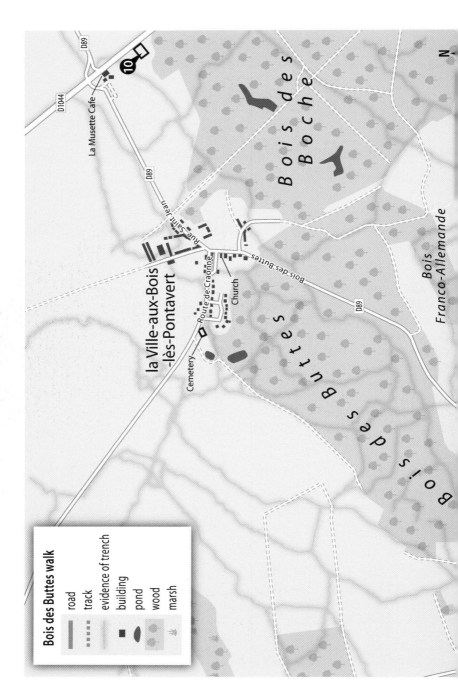

Bois des Buttes walk

road
track
evidence of trench
building
pond
wood
marsh

la Ville-aux-Bois -lès-Pontavert

Cemetery

Church

Route de Craonne

Rue Saint-Jean

La Musette Cafe

D89

D1044

D89

D89

Bois des Boche

Bois Franco-Allemande

Bois des Buttes

Bois des Buttes

N

SOISSONS MEMORIAL TO THE MISSING

The Soissons British Memorial to the Missing sits on the rise from the Pont des Anglais footbridge to the Cathedral, not far from the centre of the town. The memorial commemorates the British soldiers of the IX and XXII Corps who fell in the Battles of the Aisne and Marne in 1918 and have no known grave. It bears the following inscription:

Soissons Memorial in the 1920s.

Aux Armees Francaises et Britanniques L'Empire Britannique Reconnaissant.

When the French Armies held and drove back the enemy from the Aisne and the Marne between May and July, 1918, the 8th, 15th, 19th, 21st, 25th, 34th, 50th, 51st and 62nd Divisions of the British Armies served in the line with them and shared the common sacrifice. Here are recorded the names of 3,985 officers and men of those divisions to whom the fortune of war denied the known and honoured burial given to their comrades in death.

Soissons was chosen, after consultation with both the British and French military authorities, as the best place for the memorial. The

Imperial War Graves Commission invited architects to submit plans for a new Memorial to the Missing for the Battles of the Aisne and Marne in 1918. On St George's Day 1925 Sir Aston Webb, President of the Royal Academy and the competition's assessor, announced the winners. They were two young architects, **Verner Owen Rees** (1886-1966) and **Gordon Herbert Holt** (1892-1970), who had both served on the Western Front during the Great War.

Eric Henri Kennington (1888-1960) was invited by Rees and Holt to design a sculpture that would dominate the foreground of the memorial. Another artist,

Second Lieutenant Gordon Holt, RFA.

Edgar Allen Howes (1911-1968), designed the decorative friezes in collaboration with Kennington. This was the first work that

Kennington carried out for the Imperial War Graves Commission, but his memorial in Battersea Park to the 24th Division was already well known to the public.

Kennington arrived in Soissons in the early summer of 1927, once the site had been cleared, and carved the monument directly from stone. His sole model was made out of plaster cast, a quarter of full size. The carving took Kennington a little over a year to complete, with some help from Herbert Hart, who taught at the Royal College of Art and was mentor to Henry Moore.

Eric Kennington's model for the Soissons Memorial.

Kennington had two main aims for the 'Soissons Trinity': first, to provide his sculptured figures complete architectural harmony with the surrounding masonry; and secondly, to impart to the group a suggestion of *majesty and peace*.

The Trinity comprises three imposing British soldiers standing nine feet tall, shoulder to shoulder, wearing infantry greatcoats and full equipment. Two of the figures carry box-respirators in the 'alert' position. At the foot of the central figure a steel helmet rests against a rifle butt projecting from the ground, a common marker for the grave

Soissons Memorial figures.

of a fallen comrade in battlefield burials. Above the soldiers, the dates '1914–1918' are inscribed on the pylon against a background of interlaced rifles. On the reverse of the pylon is a design of lances and swords, used as a background to the heraldic arms of the City of Soissons. The screen is given up to the names of the 3,985 missing.

The most controversial aspect of the memorial was the 'Soissons Trinity'. These three stylised figures, inspired by Kennington's studies of Easter Island statues, were too avant-garde for some. They were a departure from the classically inspired representations of most war memorials of the period. Some critics saw the soldiers as 'resembling soulless mechanical puppets, or even worse a group of Aztec tribesmen waiting at the foot of a sacrificial altar'.

However, French observers were far more positive. The three soldiers were seen as looking typically English in *'their stockiness, bluntness, emotional restraint and disciplined passivity'*. At the unveiling ceremony, the Mayor of Soissons was impressed by the *'calm and impassive courage'* on the faces of the men, which captured the spirit that the British troops displayed in the fighting on the Western Front. Kennington himself thought that over time, once the wind and rain had worn away many of the details, the figures, so solid and enduring, would still stand impassive as a 'good ruin'.

The Missing

Amongst those commemorated here the highest-ranking casualty is **Brigadier General Cuthbert Thomas Martin DSO and Bar**, GOC

151 Brigade. In August 1914 he served in France with the Highland Light Infantry and took part in the retreat from Mons and was severely wounded at the First Battle of the Aisne in September 1914. He returned to duty in 1916 and was promoted to brigadier general in October 1917, taking command of 151 Brigade. The 50th Division history notes:

At 7 am Brigadier General Riddell was at 151 Brigade Heqadquarters with Brigadier General Martin when the enemy was reported close at hand. As the two brigadiers hurriedly left the dugout they found themselves surrounded. As they began to fight

Lieutenant Colonel Robert Frank Moore, 1/Sherwood Foresters.

their way through, the Germans were scattered by a salvo of their own shells, but one, however, unfortunately burst overhead and General Martin was instantly killed and General Riddell wounded.

Amongst the many names listed is **Lieutenant Colonel Robert Moore** of the 1/Sherwood Foresters, who until 29 May had been the only

244

Lieutenant Colonel Edward Cadman Cadman, 10/Cheshires.

battalion CO of the 8th Division who had not become a casualty. He had joined up with Brigadier General Grogan on the Bouleuse Ridge and was killed by an enemy bombardment on 30 May. Another CO whose name appears on this memorial is **Lieutenant Colonel Edward Cadman Cadman DSO,** 10/Cheshires. He was killed by low-flying aircraft fire on the Cormicy-Guyencourt road on 27 May. Yet another CO to die that day was **Lieutenant Colonel Rupert Anderson-Morshead** of 2/Devons. His story has been outlined earlier in this book. The controversial CO of the 4/Yorks, **Lieutenant Colonel Ralph Kent,** is also commemorated on this memorial. **Major James Cartland**, commanding 1/Worcesters, was killed by shellfire in the opening hours of the German attack on the first day. His daughter was the famous novelist, Barbara Cartland.

Major James Cartland, CO 1/Worcesters.

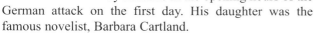

nant Colonel Ralph t, CO of 4/ Yorks.

Major Cecil Hall DSO, of 22/DLI (Pioneers), was killed defending a position south of the Aisne canal near Gernicourt Wood. A brother officer, Captain Atkinson, reported:

> *Major Hall, in the rear of his company, turned about with twenty men to lead a bayonet charge upon a party of Boche who suddenly appeared on his left. Unfortunately he received a direct hit from a shell that carried away his head, so that the charge faltered and those who survived fled away into the trees.*

Major Cecil Hall, 22/DLI (Pioneers).

Lieutenant Charles Augustus Button, one of the Croix de Guerre gunners of the 5 Battery RFA, is also commemorated here. He was last seen moving off to help his battery commander, Captain John Hamon Massey, and was killed moments later and was last seen lying dead in a trench, having been 'shot to pieces'.

Captain Norman Hessler, one of two brothers of Norwegian descent who served in 5/DLI, is commemorated here.

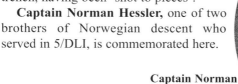

nant Charles tton, 5 Battery, igade RFA.

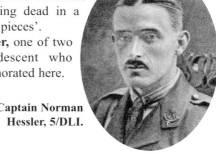

Captain Norman Hessler, 5/DLI.

Captain John Benson, 4/North Fus.

Three officers of 4/NF are commemorated. **Captain John Benson**, attached to 149 Trench Mortar Battery, led an attack on a German tank, but was killed in the effort. **Lieutenant Robert Smallwood** was killed on the same day. Two days later **Second Lieutenant John Farwell**, a Scot serving with the battalion, was badly wounded on the retreat across the Aisne and was later reported as missing. **Regimental Sergeant Major George Fewster**, also of 4/NF, was badly injured in helping to organise a defence of the Aisne canal near Concevreux. He was last seen at a regimental aid post.

Lieutenant R Smallwood, 4 Fus.

The **Reverend George Bishop,** attached 6/NF, was reported killed in action on 27 May 1918. It seems likely that he was killed in the opening salvos of the German bombardment. He had been appointed Chaplain 4th Class in May 1917 and was assigned to the Northumberland Fusiliers.

Lieutenant John Farwell, 4/North Fus.

RSM George [ ] 4/North Fus.

Sergeant William A 'Tommy' Fiske was a professional football player, and for most of his career he played in goal for Blackpool, making 217 appearances. In 1914 he joined Nottingham Forest. When war broke out he was one of the first to join up and served initially with the Norfolk Regiment. He was twice wounded and promoted to sergeant. On 20th September 1917 he was posted to 8/Borders and was killed on 27 May near the town of Fismes, south of the Aisne.

The Reverend George Bishop attached 6/Nor[ ]

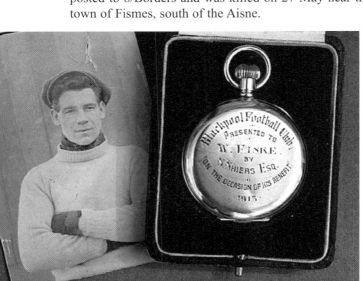

Sergeant 'Tomm[ ] Fiske, 8/Borders

AISNE 1918 BRITISH CEMETERIES

The cemeteries considered here do not form part of the tour itineraries.

Cemeteries to the north of the Aisne

Sissonne British Cemetery

This cemetery, which is roughly twenty kilometres from Laon on the Reims road, was constructed after the Armistice and has burials from the Battles of the Aisne and from German military cemeteries. Many of the men died of wounds in German captivity.

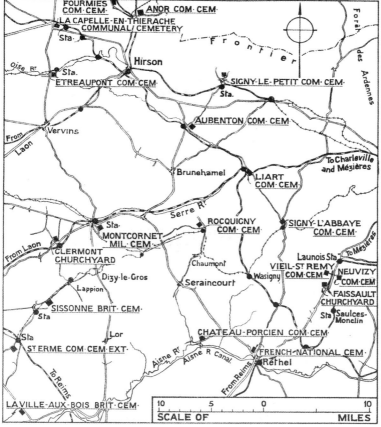

Sissonne Group of CWGC cemeteries.

Sissonne British Cemetery.

Those buried here include:

Private Rowland Walsh (O14), of 7/Leicesters and a resident of Higham, near Colne in Lancashire. He was taken prisoner on 27 May, badly wounded. Nevertheless, he wrote home on 7 June from a German hospital: 'I am doing well under the circumstances. We cannot grumble at the food we get'. Unfortunately his condition deteriorated and he died on 10 June, aged 39.

Another Colne man, **Private Thomas Sarginson** (O6) of 1/Lincolnshire Regiment, died on 1 June, probably from wounds received.

Corporal Thomas John Goulder (N13) from Greenford, Middlesex, who served with B Battery CCLI Brigade Royal Field Artillery. He was killed on 27 May.

Private Thomas Sarginson, 1/Lincolns.

Private Rowland Walsh 7/Leicesters.

248

Corporal Thomas Goulder, CCLI Brigade RFA.

Moncornet British Cemetery.

Montcornet Military Cemetery

The cemetery was used by the Germans to bury prisoners of war (PoW) from the nearby Montcornet Hospital between May and October 1918.

From 1927 to 1938 bodies of British soldiers, mainly from the Aisne battlefields to the east, were concentrated here. A large number of these date from September 1914. There are also twenty burials from the Second World War.

Commemorated here is **Second Lieutenant Harold William Field** (Sp Mem No 1) of IX Corps Cyclist Battalion (formerly West Yorkshire Regiment) killed on 27 May. It is possible that he was buried in Crugny Churchyard but his body was lost and now he is commemorated in the form of a Special Memorial.

Second Lieutenant Harold W Field, IX Corps Cyclists.

St Erme British Cemetery.

St. Erme Communal Cemetery Extension

Ramecourt, the small settlement to the north, was a holding 'cage' for prisoners captured during the Aisne battle before they were moved on to other PoW camps. Of the 2,000 men housed in this camp in May there were only 292 still alive by October. A number of the dead are buried in this cemetery. Most of the men buried in St. Erme are from the Yorkshire, East Yorkshire and Durham Light Infantry battalions associated with the 50th (Northumbrian) Division.

German tanks 'Liesel' and 'Lotte' at St Erme; most tanks involved in the 27 May attack detrained here.

Vailly Cemetery.

Vailly British Cemetery

This cemetery was built after the Armistice when burials were brought in from other cemeteries and from the battlefields. Most of the 670 burials are from the First Battle of the Aisne, but over sixty date from the summer of 1918. Two notable burials from this period are two members of the Friends' Ambulance Unit (FAU). **Orderly Hugo Harrison Jackson** (I AA18), a devout Quaker from Kendal in Westmoreland, had served with the FAU since November 1914. This unit provided help for the *Services Sanitaires Anglaises* (SSA) of the French Army. On the morning of 27 May, when helping

**Orderly Hugo
Jackson, Friends'
Ambulance Unit.**

to move injured French troops to a hospital at Braine, south of the Aisne, his ambulance was hit by a shell. The driver, **Orderly Norman Gripper** (I AA15), was killed instantly, and he too is buried in this cemetery. Hugo Jackson died en route to a dressing station. Both men were awarded the Croix de Guerre. They were both originally buried in the grounds of a chateau at Mont Notre Dame. After the war their bodies were reinterred here.

**Orderly Norman
Gripper, FAU.**

The body of **Private Fred Ashmore** (I AA20), 6/DLI, was also moved here from Mont Notre Dame. He received a gunshot wound to the shoulder on the morning of the German attack. He was taken to a British Casualty Clearing Station, but it was captured on 28 May. Fred later died of his wounds in the care of the Germans on 17 July and his body was moved to Vailly sometime in the 1920s. **Private George Collins** (III A29), 2/East Lancs, a Lewis gunner from Manchester is also here.

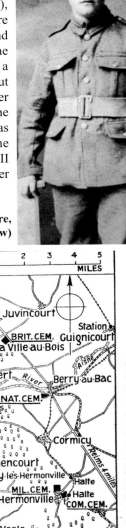

Private George Collins, 2/East Lancs.

Private Fred Ashmore, 6/DLI. (F Ashmore, nephew)

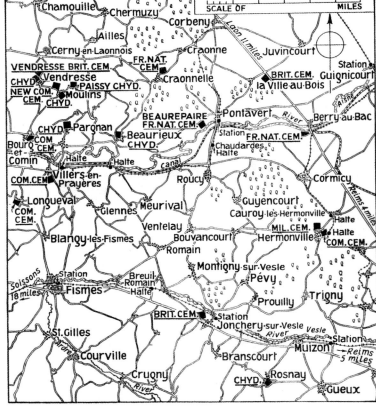

Vendresse group of cemeteries, including Jonchery British Cemetery.

Cemeteries to the south of the Aisne

The countryside of the Haute Marne is one of rolling hills and the absence of hedgerows and few trees suited the needs of mobile warfare. It helps explain the comparatively rapid advance of the Germans after crossing the Aisne on 27 May and its pursuit of the IX Corps to the Marne. But it was, in Sidney Rogerson's phrase, 'the last of the ebb', and subsequent fighting here in July 1918 marked the turning point in the war, with Allied troops now taking to the offensive, during the Second Battle of the Marne. As a result the cemeteries in this area contain casualties from both battles that ebbed and flowed across this distinctive landscape in the summer of 1918.

Captain John Hamon Massey.

Jonchery Sur Vesle British Cemetery

The cemetery was made after the Armistice by the concentration of graves from other cemeteries. It was designed by Sir Edwin Lutyens and John Truelove.

Among those buried here are:

Captain John Hamon Massey MC (I H15), 5 (Gibraltar Battery), XLV Brigade Royal Field Artillery. For his outstanding leadership on 27 May he was Mentioned in Despatches and was awarded the Croix de Guerre with Palmes. His body was discovered in 1927 and he was reinterred here.

Lieutenant John Pippet.

Second Lieutenant John Gilbert Pippet (I F21) 1/Lincolns, formerly of the East Yorkshire Regiment, who was killed on 29 May when his unit was falling back towards the Marne.

Orderly Colin Priestman (I E10) of the Friends' Ambulance Unit, who was killed in August 1918.

Orderly Colin Priestman, FAU.

Romigny Churchyard

This is the most southerly of the cemeteries associated with the 1918 Aisne battle and contains four British graves dating from May 1918.

Marfaux British Cemetery.

Marfaux British Cemetery

The majority of the men buried here are associated with the Second Battle of the Marne, July 1918. The Aisne casualties are from all the divisions of IX Corps, demonstrating the hastiness of the retreat and the mixed nature of the formations that fell back towards the Marne.

Serjeant James Armstrong DCM, MM (I AA1) of 8/DLI is amongst those buried here. He won the DCM for actions carried out 22 May as part of a trench raid. He was recuperating in the transport lines when his vehicle was hit by shellfire on 27 May.

Serjeant J Armst... DCM MM, 1/8 D...

Serjeant J Armstrong's, headstone.

Albert Hiram 'Bertie' Harman (V H7) was killed towards the end of the battle on 6 June. He hailed from Rotherfield in Sussex and was a private in the Royal Army Medical Corps, part of 58th Field Ambulance.

Another man from the RAMC, **Private William Nutter** (I D4) from Burnley is also buried here. His Commanding Officer wrote:

He was badly wounded whilst in the performance of his duty, and was evacuated to No. 48 Clearing Station. I regret I have no further news of his movements after 27 May. Your son was one of the best men under my command. He was a great loss to this unit.

Private Bert Harman, RAMC.

te William Nutter, eld Amb. RAMC.

It is believed he died as a prisoner of war on 29 May. Another young soldier buried here is **Private James Davis** (I AA6) from 10/Worcesters, who died from wounds received on 31 May. He had just turned nineteen and was from near Alvechurch, Worcestershire.

Private William Webster (VII F1), 9/Cheshires, fought in all the Spring Offensives of 1918 and was killed in the fighting for Mount Bligny, 5 June.

Private William B Webster, 9/Cheshires.

Private James Davis, 10/Worcesters.

Chambrecy British Cemetery.

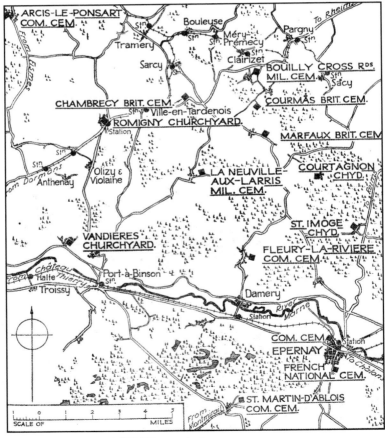

Chambrecy group of CWGC cemeteries.

Chambrecy British Cemetery

There are 128 burials associated with the Aisne 1918, the vast majority from units of the 19th (Western) Division.

Captain David Turner (VC 2), 4/NF, helped organize the defence of the bridge across the Aisne at Concevreux on 27 May, allowing other members of the battalion to escape. Three days later, at Romigny, where he was in charge of 149 Company (part of a composite Brigade of the 50th Division), he was involved in another defensive action. This time his role was to

Captain David Turner, 4/North Fus.

prevent the enemy taking the village. At 2.30 pm the German infantry attacked. There was considerable rifle and machine gun fire; Captain Turner went to reconnoitre front line positions and was never seen alive again. **Private Alfred March** (VC 1), 21st Division Machine Gun Corps, is buried alongside Captain Turner. He had formerly fought with the Leicesters.

Headstones of Private Alfred March and Captain David Turner.

ate Alfred March, with cross, 21st hine Gun Company.

Captain Ernest Thurgood (II C3) was killed in action on 31 May serving in 9/Cheshires. He enlisted in the Royal Fusiliers in 1914 and was later transferred to the 16/Cheshire. By April 1918 he was acting Lieutenant Colonel. The historian of the Cheshire Regiment writes:

Captain Ernest F Thurgood, 9/Cheshires.

About mid day (31 May), German artillery and machine guns opened on the battalion. They had excellent observation of our positions from the high ground immediately south of Sarcy, west of the Sarcy-Chambrecy road, on to which their infantry had got opposite to the French on our left, and also from the high ground south east of Lhéry. Their fire grew in intensity until mid afternoon, when the left of our front in the valley was a perfect inferno of high explosives and machine gun fire, against which our hastily improvised cover was useless. Most of the officers were killed or wounded. In particular we lost Captain Thurgood and Lieutenant Gibbs, both excellent and conscientious officers whom we could very ill afford to lose.

Captain Ernest F Thurgood. Relaxing in a dug out c. 1917.

Bouilly Cross Roads Military Cemetery.

Bouilly Cross Roads Military Cemetery

This cemetery, deep in the heart of the Champagne countryside, was started in 1918 to accommodate British, French, Italian and German soldiers. After the Armistice the casualties of the other countries were removed and the cemetery became a resting place solely for British graves.

There are just over 200 burials here, including those of eleven men who fell in the Aisne 1918, most of whom were from the 19th (Western) Division.

Courmas British Cemetery

It commemorates over 200 men, mostly from the battles of July 1918. Four men buried here were killed in the Aisne fighting of May and June. Two of the casualties are from 2/Wilts.

Courmas British Cemetery.

Arcis Le Ponsart Communal Cemetery

This small cemetery contains the graves of sixty-four French soldiers and, in the north east section, the graves of two British soldiers from the Army Veterinary Corps and one from the Royal Engineers killed on 27 May.

19th (Western) Division Memorial

This remote memorial is seldom visited, tucked away in the Champagne countryside overlooking the **Montagne de Bligny**, behind the impressive Italian cemetery near Chambrecy British Cemetery. In

Italian Cemetery at Bligny.

A LA MEMOIRE TOUJOURS GLORIEUSE DES OFFICIERS ET SOLDATS
DE LA 19ème DIVISION BRITANNIQUE MORTS AU CHAMP D'HONNEUR
EN CHAMPAGNE MAI-JUIN 1918 CE MONUMENT EST ERIGE
SUR LA MONTAGNE DE BLIGNY REPRISE ET TENUE PAR

LA 19e DIVISION
LE 6 JUIN 1918

19th Division Memorial detail.

many respects this memorial marks the end of the Aisne battle of 1918 as it commemorates the last action on 6 June 1918 when 8/North Staffords, 9/Cheshires and 1/4 Shropshires, all from the 19th (Western) Division, seized Bligny from the Germans at 7 pm that day.

(Western) Division Memorial Bligny.

The memorial is in the form of a simple cross, with the divisional emblem, the butterfly, engraved on the upper section. The division has two similar memorials: at La Boisselle on the Somme; and near Messines, south of Ypres.

GERMAN CEMETERIES ASSOCIATED WITH THE AISNE 1918

Mons-en-Laonnois German Military Cemetery

Cerny-en-Laonnois German Military Cemetery

Sissonne German Military Cemetery

Soupir German Military Cemetery

Montaigu I German Military Cemetery

Loivre German Military Cemetery

Bligny German Military Cemetery

Marfaux German Military Cemetery

264

ORDER OF BATTLE
OF BRITISH FORCES:
IX Corps
(Battle of the Aisne, 27 May-6 June 1918)

8th Division: Major General W C G Heneker

23rd Brigade: Brigadier General W St G Grogan

2/Devons
2/Middlesex
2/West Yorks

24th Brigade: Brigadier General R Haig (Wounded)

1 Worcesters
1 Sherwood Foresters
2 Northamptonshire
1/ Worcesters
1/ Sherwoods
1/ Northamptons

25th Brigade: Brigadier General R H Husey (Killed In Action)

2/East Lancs
2/Berks
2/Rifle Brigade

R F A Brigades:

XXXIII
XLV

Field Coys. R E:

2
15
490

Pioneers:

22/DLI

21st Division: Major General D G M Campbell

62nd Brigade: Brigadier General G H Gater
12/13 NF
1/Lincs
2/Lincs

64th Brigade: Brigadier General H R Headlam
1/East Yorks
9/KOYLI
15/DLI

110th Brigade: Brigadier General H R Cumming
6/Leicesters
7/Leicesters
8/Leicesters

R F A Brigades:
XCIV
XCV

Field Coys. R E:
97
98
126

Pioneers:
14/NF

25th Division: Major General Sir E G T Bainbridge

7th Brigade: Brigadier General C J Griffin
10/Cheshire
4/South Staffords
1/Wilts

74th Brigade: Brigadier General H M Craigie Halkett
11/ Lancs Fus
3/Worcesters
9/Loyal North Lancs

75th Brigade: Brigadier General A A Kennedy
11/Cheshire
8/Borders
2/South Lancs

R F A Brigades:
CX
CXII

Field Coys. R E:
105
106
130

Pioneers:
6/South Wales Borders

50th (Northumbrian) Division: Major General H C Jackson

149th Brigade: Brigadier General E P A Riddell (Wounded)
4/NF
5/NF
6/NF

150th Brigade: Brigadier General H C Rees (Prisoner of War)
1/4 East Yorks
4/Yorks
5/Yorks

151st Brigade: Brigadier General C T Martin (Killed in Action)
5/DLI
6/DLI
8/DLI

R F A Brigades:
CCL
CCLI

Field Coys. R E
7

446
447

Pioneers:
7th Durham

19th Division: Major General G D Jeffreys

56th Brigade: Brigadier General R M Heath
9/Cheshires
1 /4 Shropshires
8/ North Staffs

57th Brigade: Brigadier General T A Cubitt
10/ Warwicks
8/ Gloucesters
10 /Worcesters

58th Brigade: Brigadier General A E Glasgow
9/Welch Fus
9/Welch
2/Wilts

R F A Brigades:
LXXXVII
LXXXVIII

Field Coys. R E
81
82
94

Pioneers:
5/S Wales Borders

ORDER OF BATTLE
OF GERMAN INFANTRY UNITS:
27th May 1918

Seventh Army:
General von Boehn

Corps von Conta

10th Division: Attack Division

6th Grenadier Regiment
47th Infanterie Regiment
398th Infanterie Regiment

28th Division: Attack Division

40th Infanterie Regiment
109th Baden Leib Grenadiers
110th Baden Leib Grenadiers

5th Garde Division: Attack Division

3rd Garde Grenadiers (Queen Elisabeth Regiment)
3rd Foot Garde
20th Reserve Regiment (3rd Brandenburg)

103rd Division: Trench Division

32nd Infanterie Regiment
71st Infanterie Regiment
144th Infanterie Regiment

36th Division

• Only one battalion of the 128th Infanterie Regiment in the line on
  27th May 1918

Corps von Schmettow

50th Division: Attack Division (Westphalia)

39th Fusilier Regiment
53rd Infanterie Regiment
158th Infanterie Regiment

52nd Division: Attack Division (Baden)

111th Infanterie Regiment
169th Infanterie Regiment
170th Infanterie Regiment

7th Reserve Division (Prussian Saxony: Part of Thuringia)

36th Reserve Infanterie Regiment
66th Reserve Infanterie Regiment

First Army:
General von Boehn; General Fritz von Below

33rd Reserve Division

364th Infanterie Regiment
67th Reserve Infanterie Regiment
130th Reserve Infanterie Regiment

GENERAL INDEX

Blücher, Operation, 31
British Field Hospital, Mont Notre
    Dame, 166, 251–2
Gneisenau, Operation, 182
Last of the Ebb, The, 115, 203, 220,
    253

Mount Hermel-Trench Déhard Line,
    218
Nivelle Offensive, 20, 193, 205,
    215, 219, 224

INDEX OF UNITS

British Army;
  Brigades;
    7, 161, 165, 202
    23, 25, 71, 99–117, 127, 170,
        198, 203, 230, 233–4, 237
    24, 25, 99, 107, 117–20, 124–5,
        127
    25, 24, 99, 118–26, 191, 202,
        205
    62, 136, 137–9, 147, 207–208
    64, 147–56, 208
    74, 162, 165
    75, 162, 164–5, 168, 203
    149, 23–4, 54, 62, 70–90, 92,
        98, 102, 107–108, 131, 198,
        203, 219, 237
    150, 18, 24, 34–52, 58, 62, 92,
        98, 196–7, 209, 212–25, 267
    151, 18, 24, 34, 52–69, 71, 73,
        81, 90, 93, 98, 197, 219, 244,
        267
    110 (Leicestershire), 18, 135,
        139–47, 151, 159, 171, 208,
        248, 257, 266
    45 RFA, 127, 230, 245
    CCL (I Northumbrian) Brigade,
        34, 91–8, 267
    CX RFA Brigade, 159
    CXII RFA Brigade, 159, 267
    XCIV Royal Field Artillery,
        155, 178, 266
    XCV Royal Field Artillery,
        155, 266
    XLV Royal Field Artillery, 109,
        116, 126–34, 230–2, 253,
        265

    Brigade, XXXIII Royal Field
        Artillery, 126–34, 265
  British Expeditionary Force
    (BEF), 17, 28, 182, 184
  Corps;
    IX, 13, 15, 19, 21–2, 26, 28,
        32, 72, 86, 105, 109, 115,
        117, 147, 150, 153–4, 157,
        167–8, 177–8, 180–1, 189,
        222, 241, 249, 253–4, 265
    XXII, 182, 241
  Divisions;
    8th Division, 13, 15, 18, 24–5,
        29, 34, 54, 58, 66, 71, 78,
        80–1, 99–134, 139–40,
        143–4, 154–9, 161–4, 173–4,
        179, 181, 191, 198–200, 206,
        210, 219, 237, 241, 245, 265
    15th Division, 241
    19th (Western) Division, 259,
        261
    19th Division, 13, 15, 169,
        173–5, 178–82, 219, 241,
        257, 259–61, 268
    21st Division, 13, 15, 18, 25–6,
        135–56, 158–9, 162, 164–6,
        168, 171, 179–80, 182, 199,
        206, 208, 219, 241, 257, 266
    25th Division, 13, 15, 18, 21,
        33, 68, 72, 81, 86, 118, 139,
        140, 158–9, 161, 164–6, 168,
        173–4, 179, 181, 192, 241,
        265–6
    34th Division, 241
    50th (Northumbrian) Division,
        13, 15, 18, 21–4, 29, 34,

271

INDEX OF PEOPLE

INDEX OF PLACES

279